Coloring Books for Kids & Toddlers

this coloring book
belongs to:

____

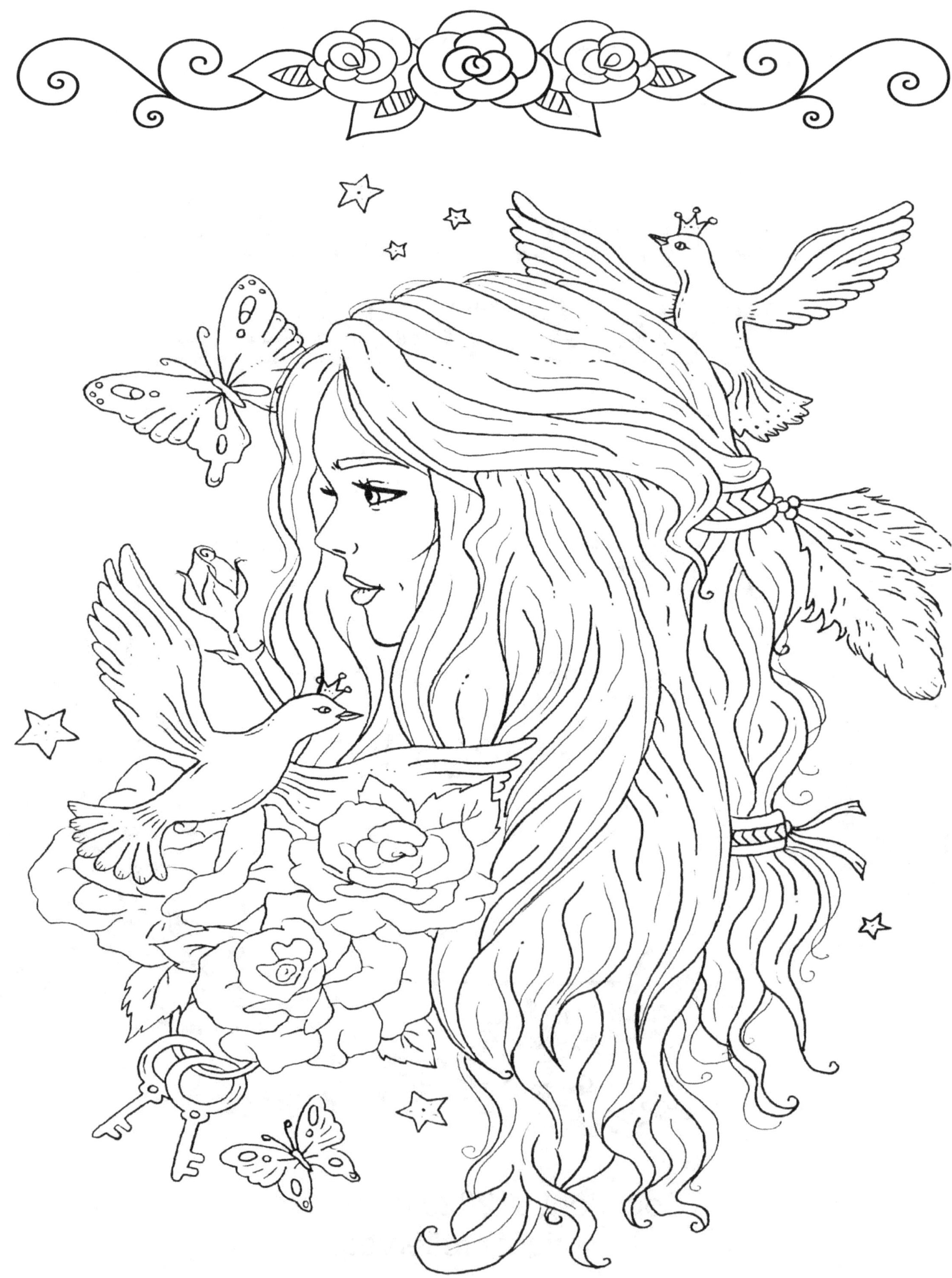

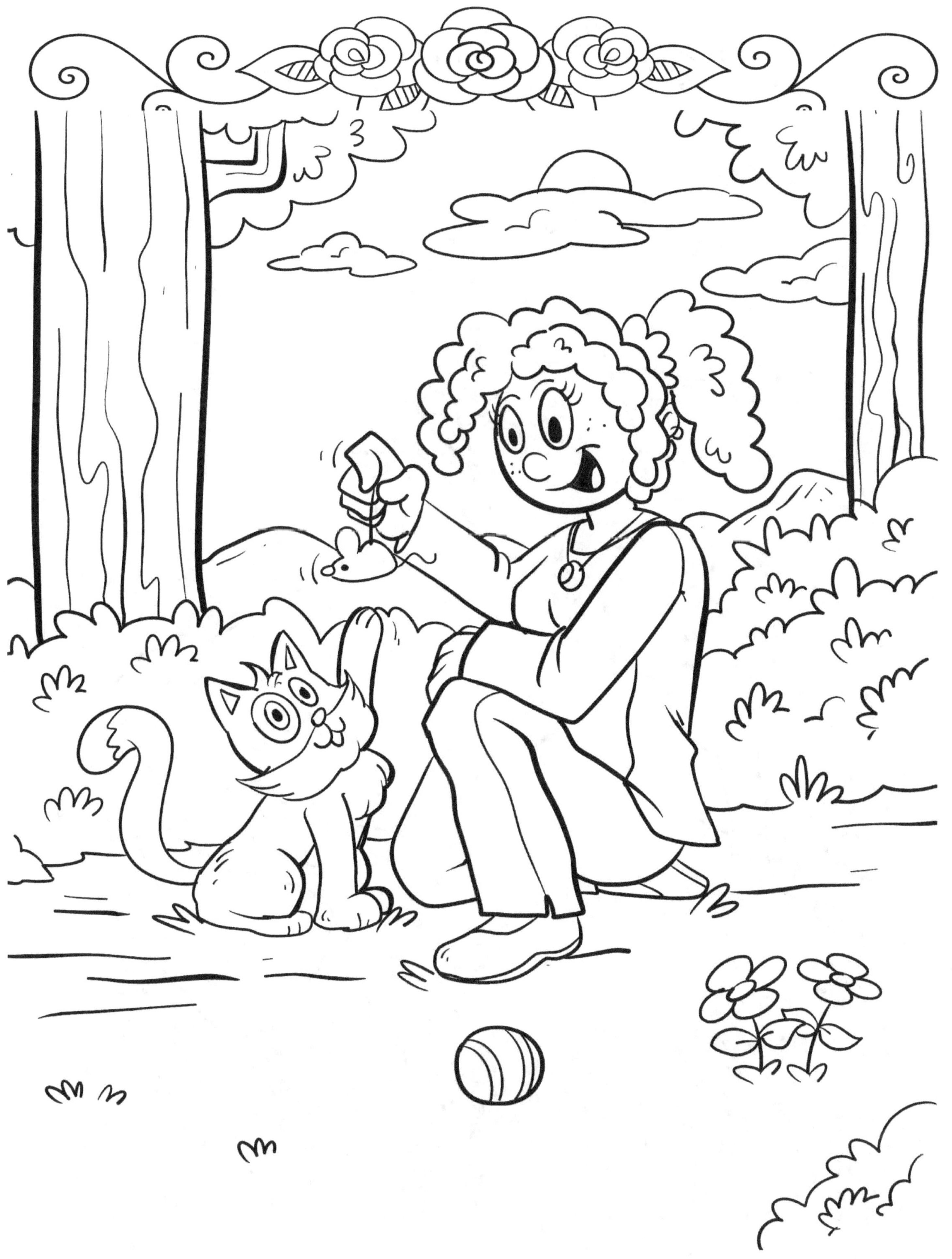

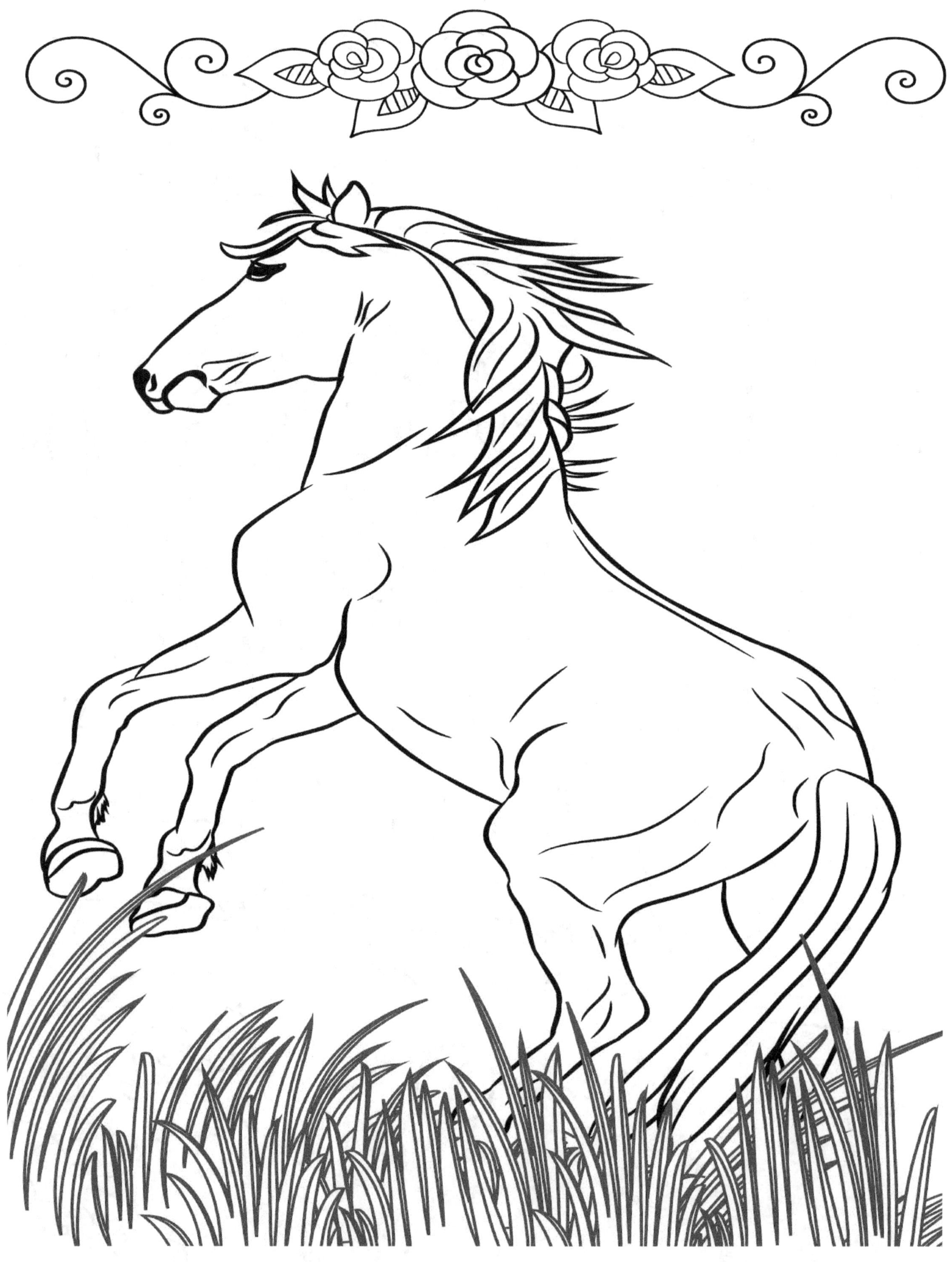

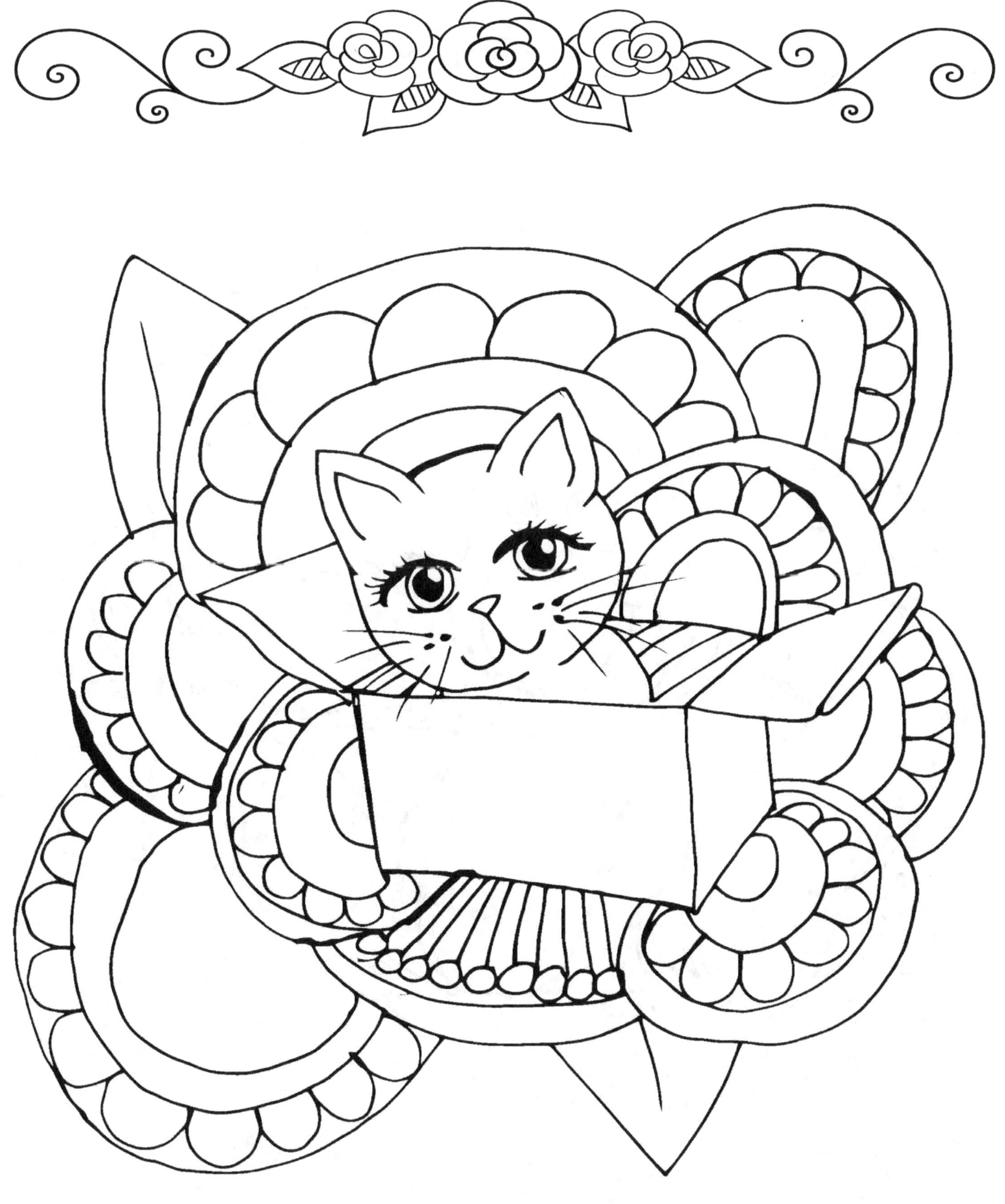

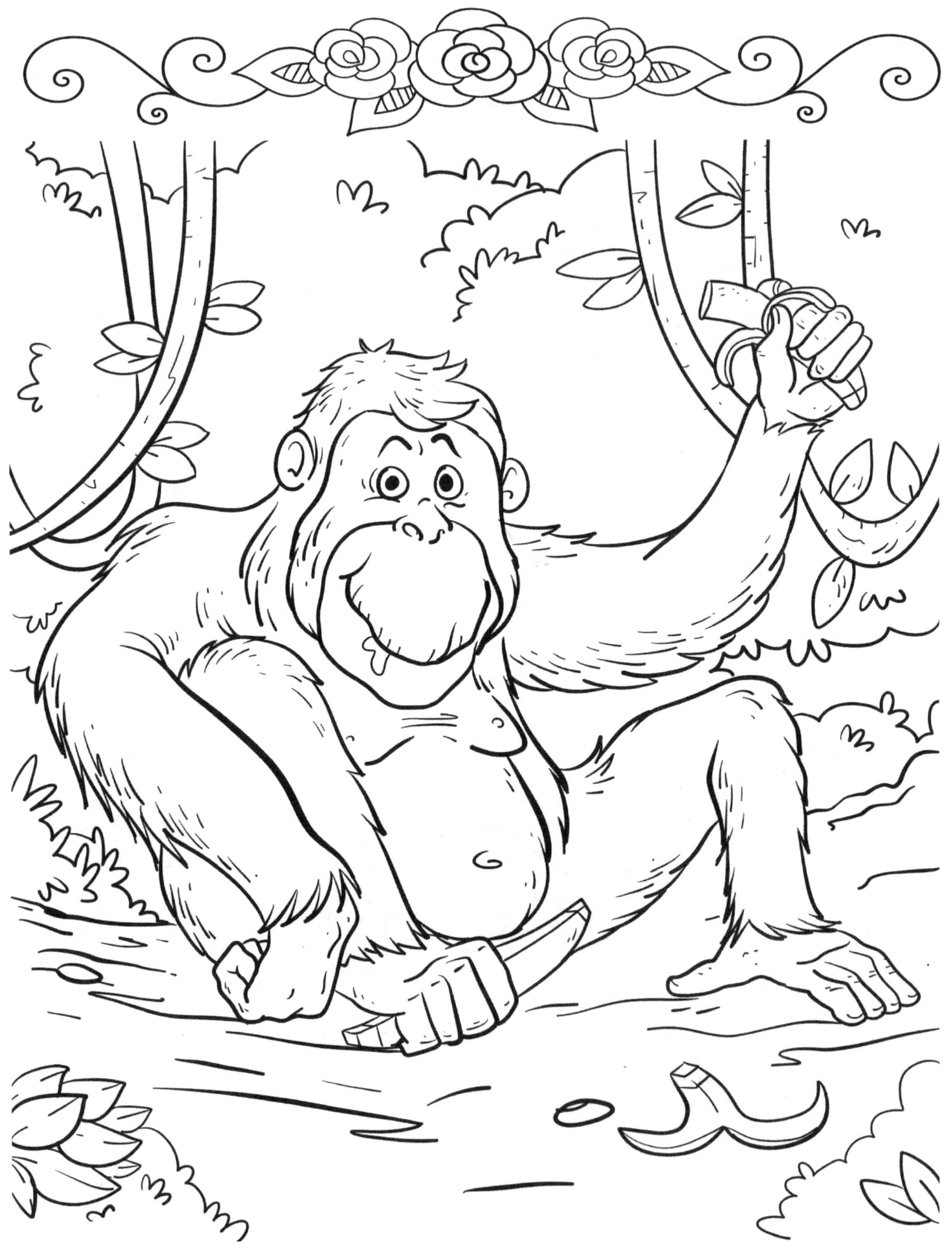

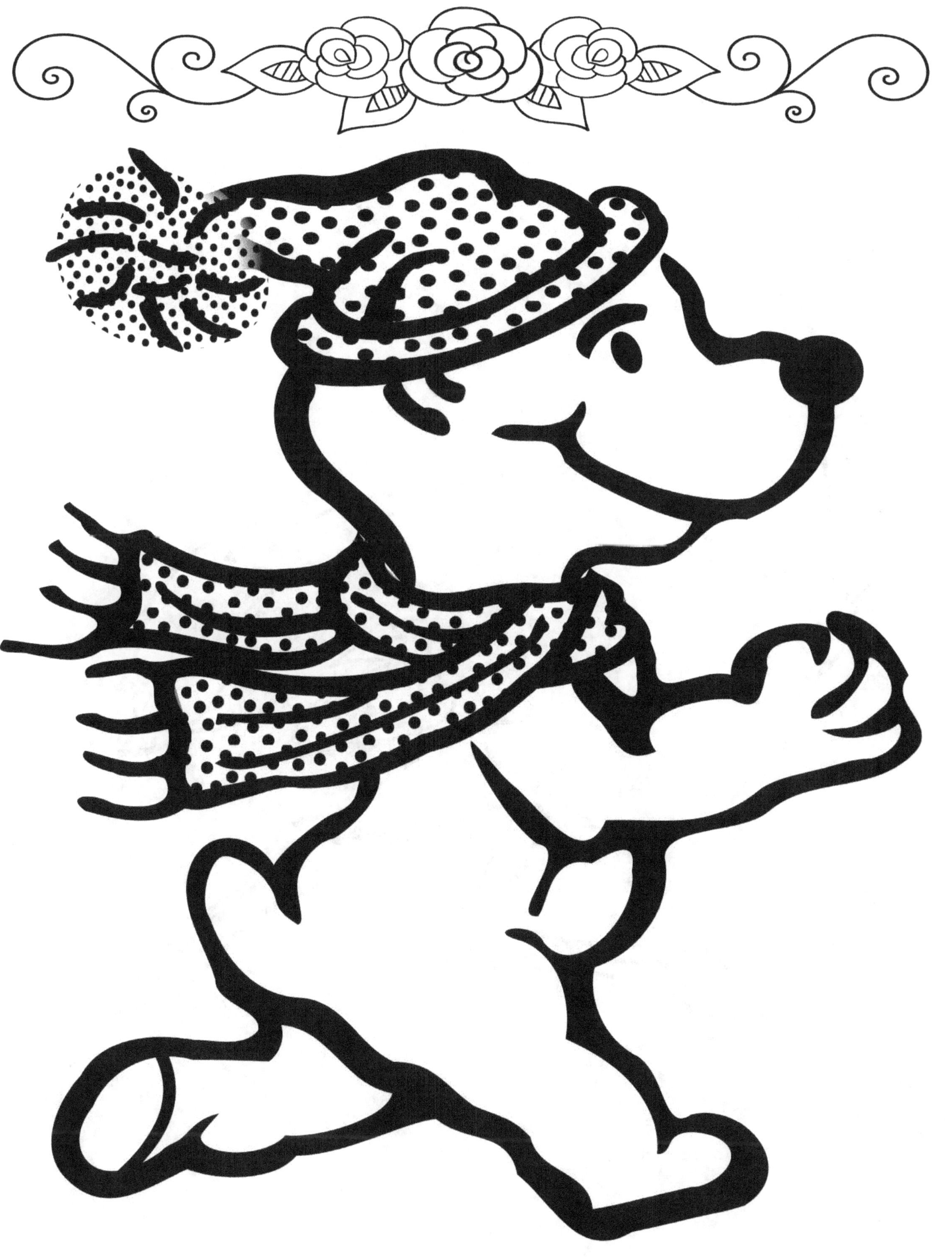

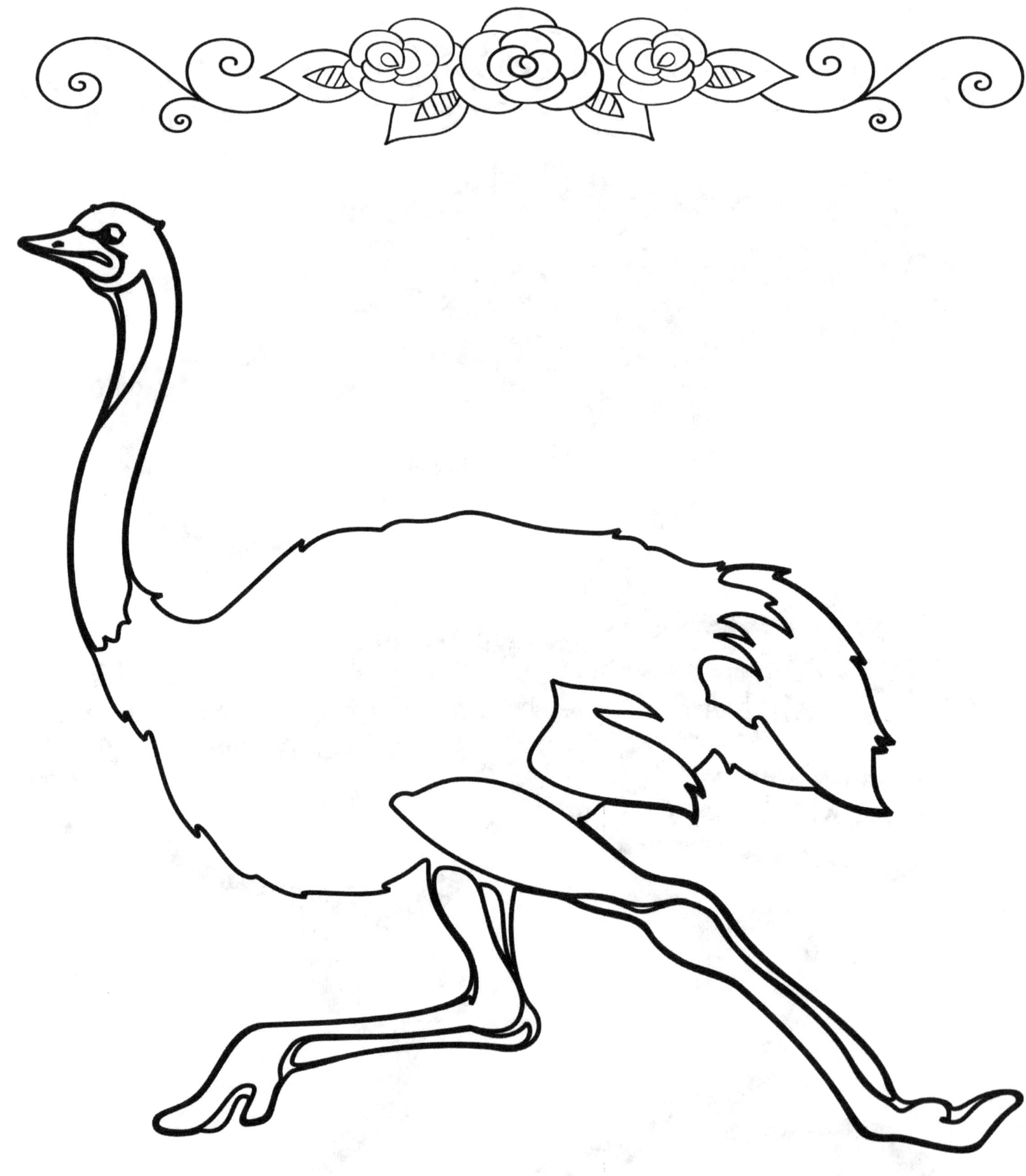

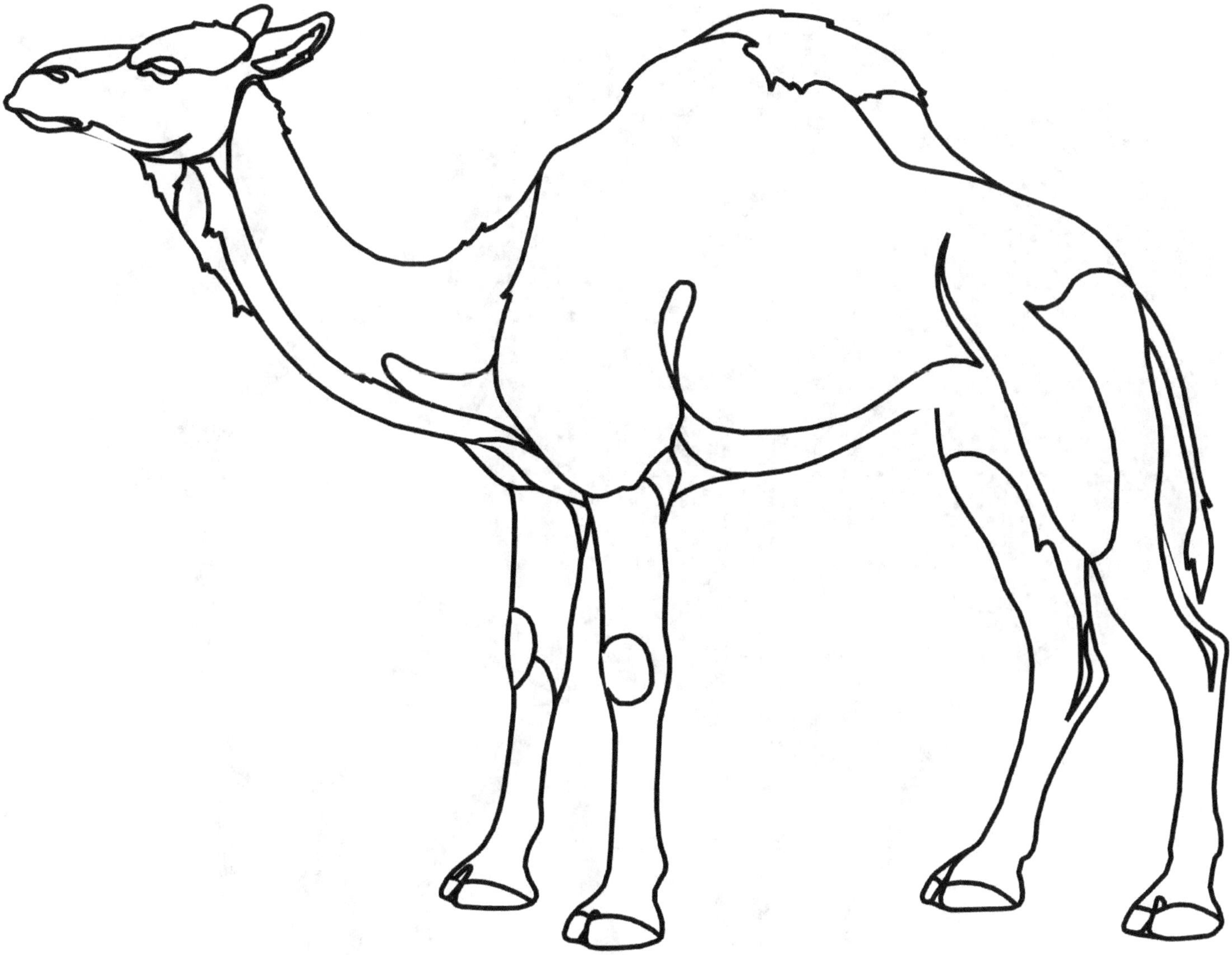

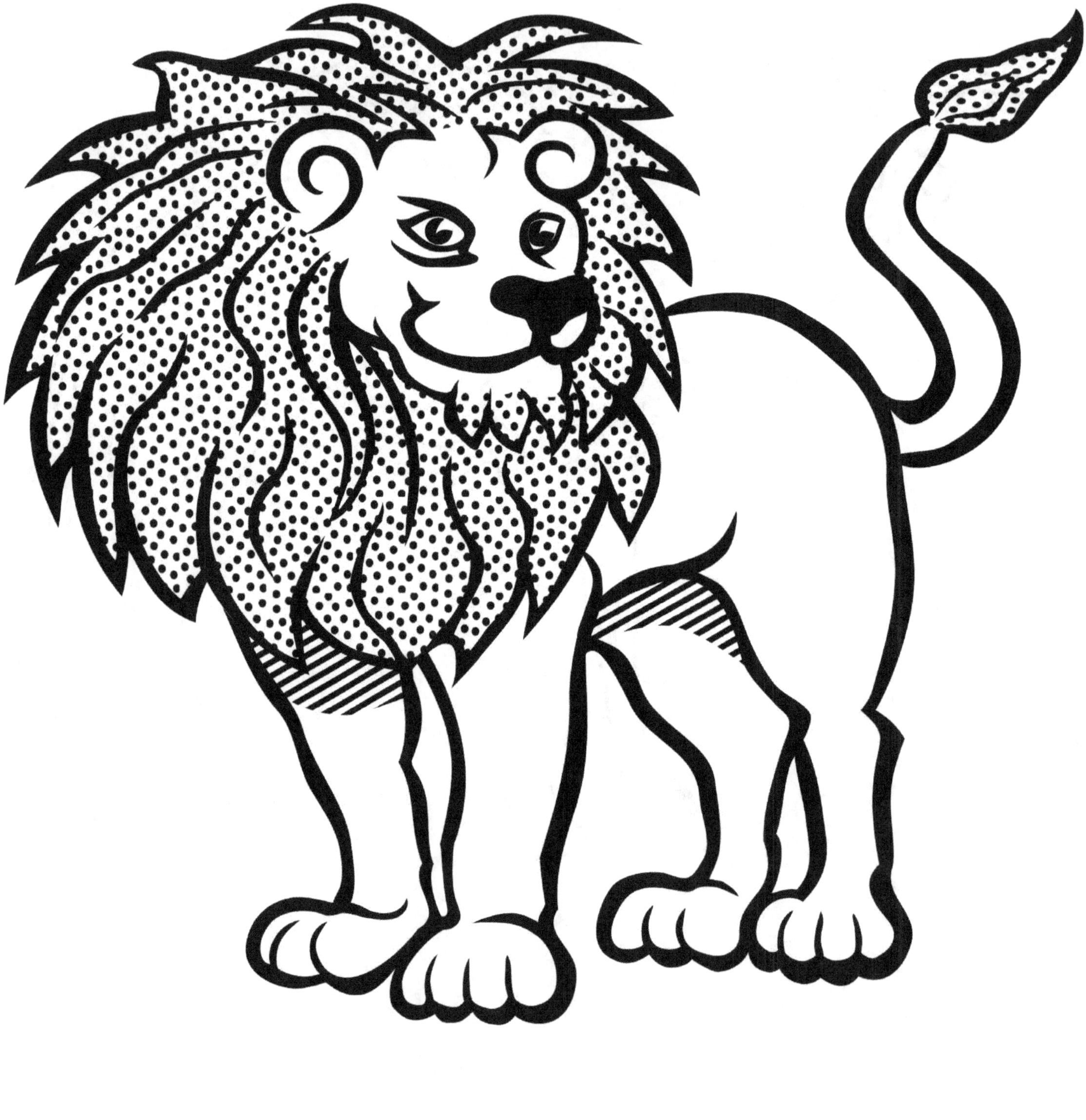

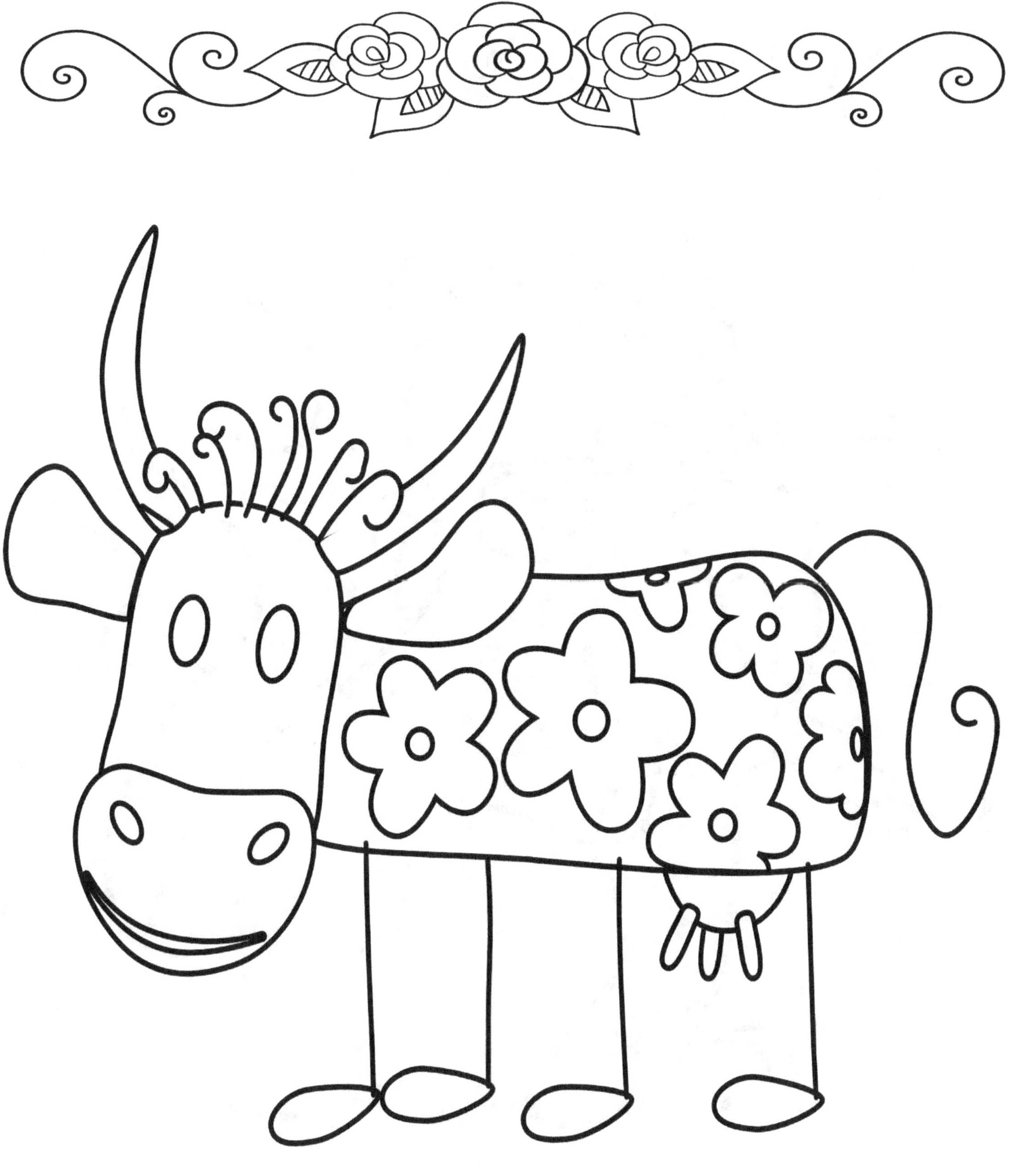

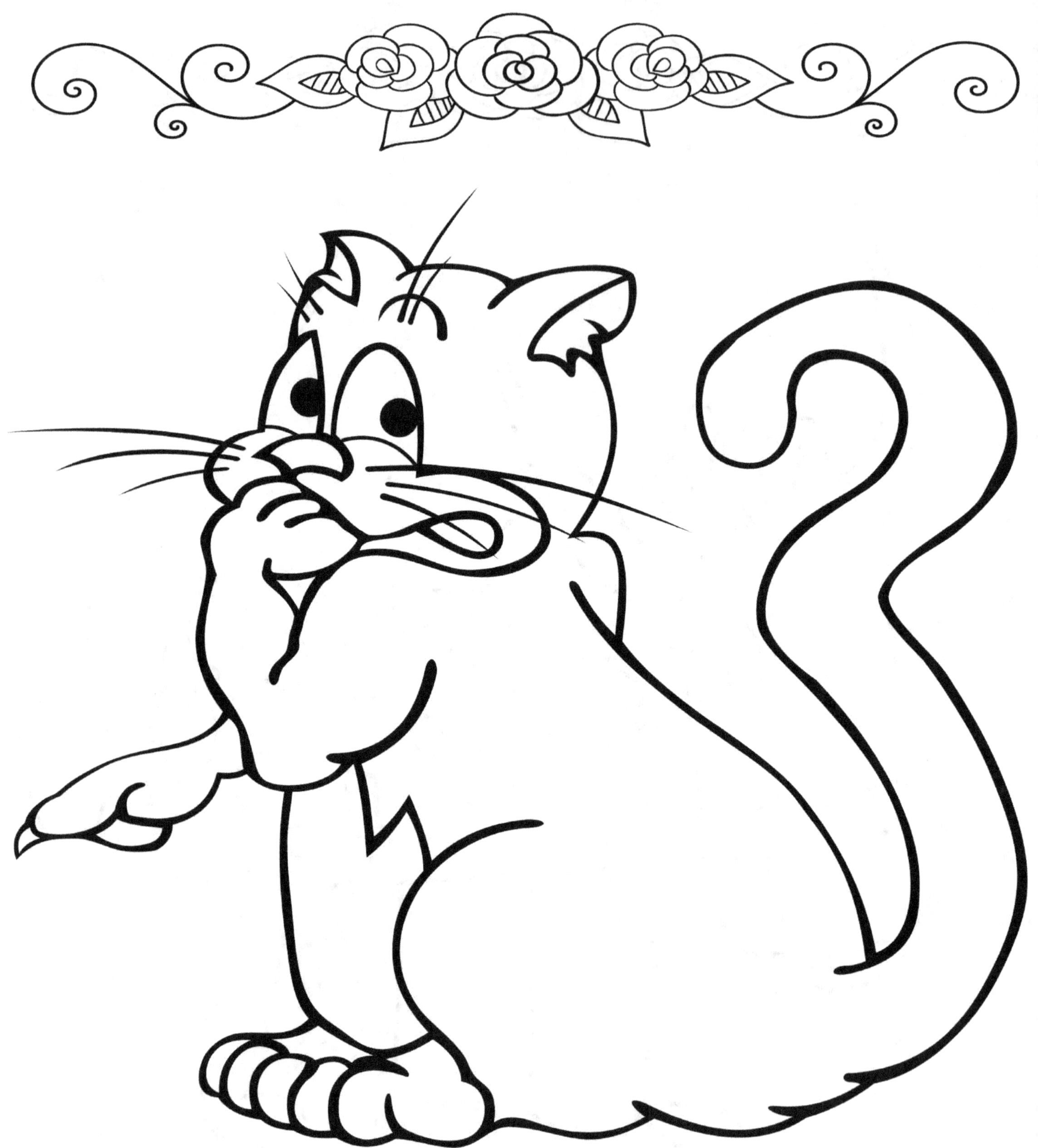

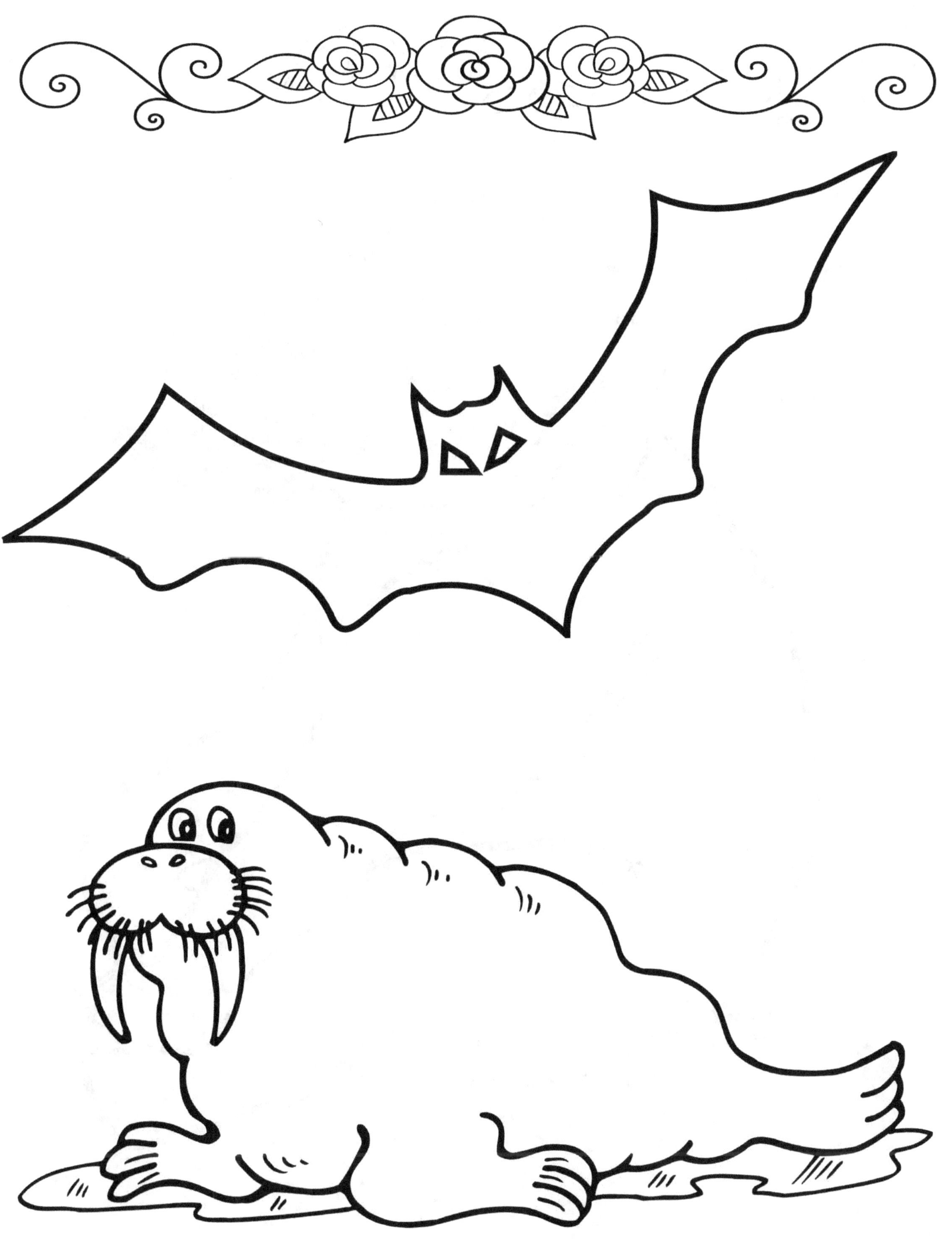

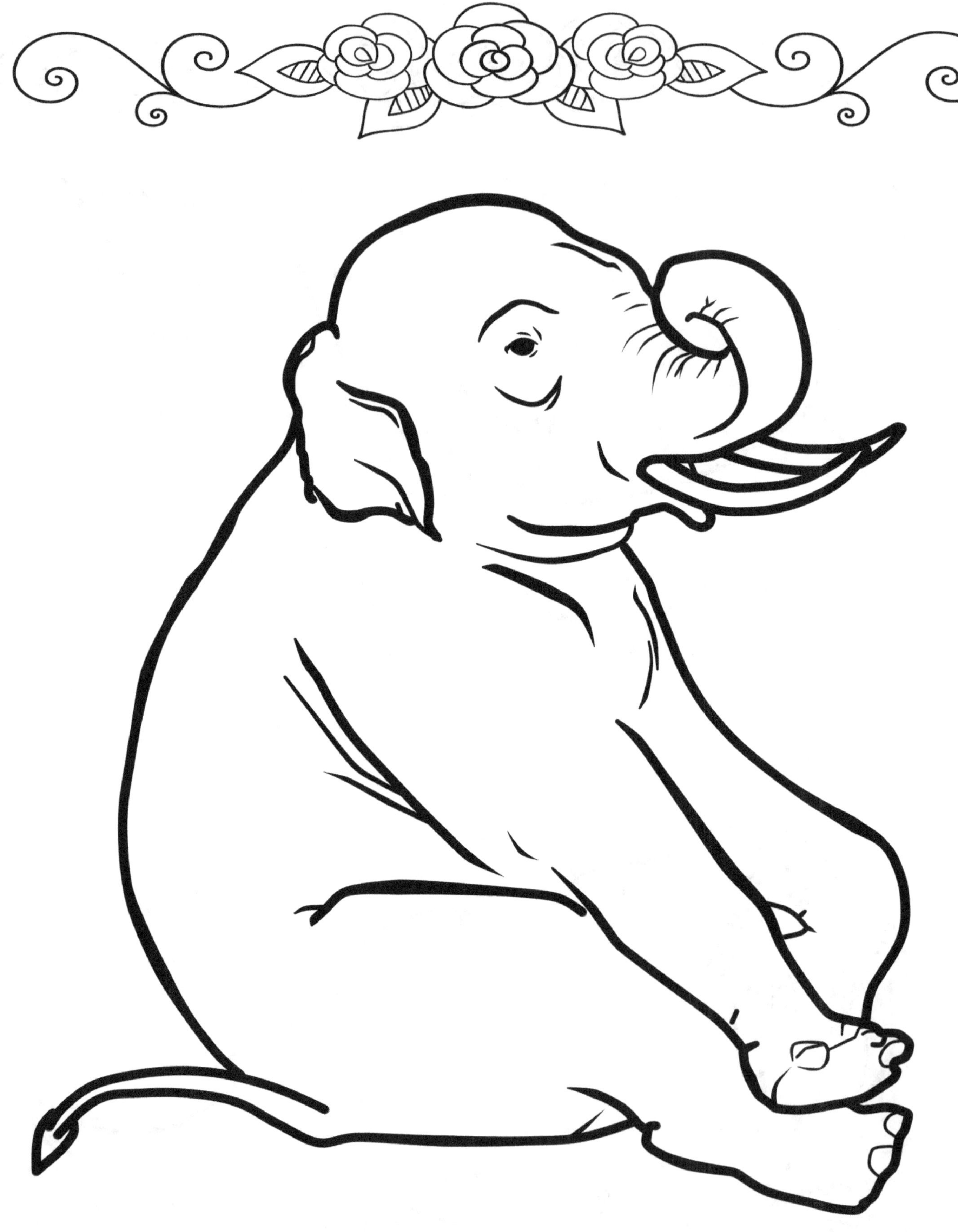

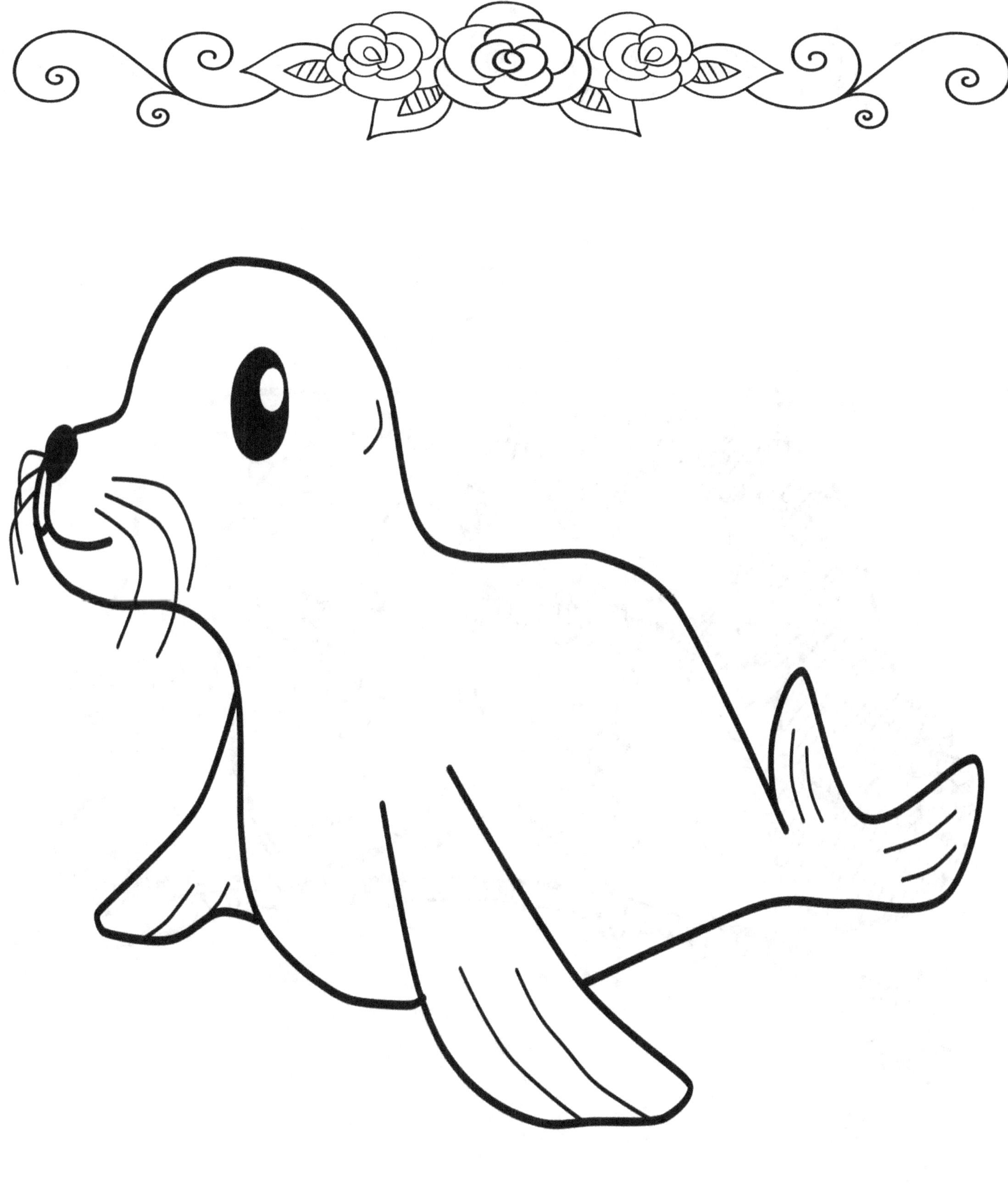

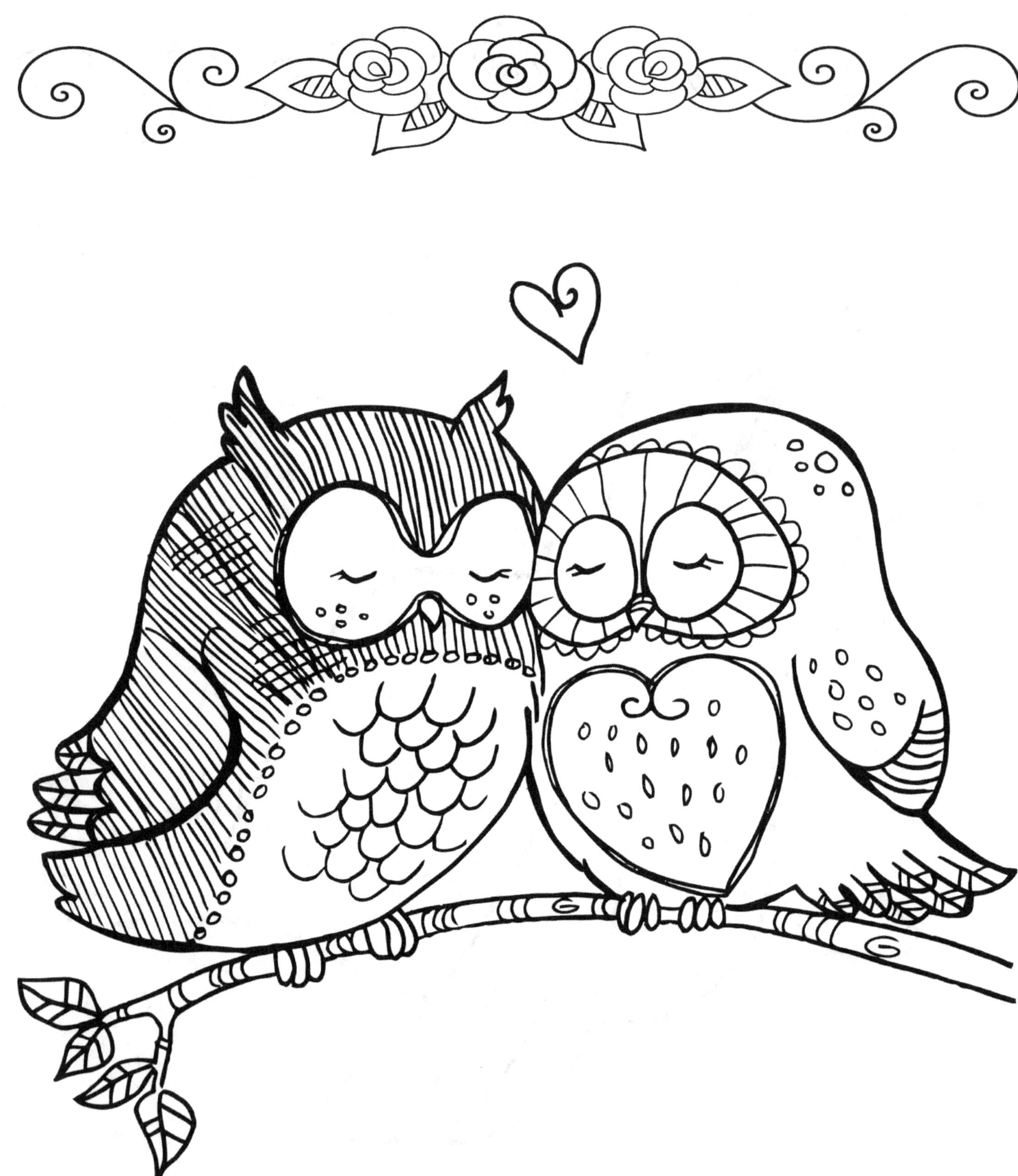

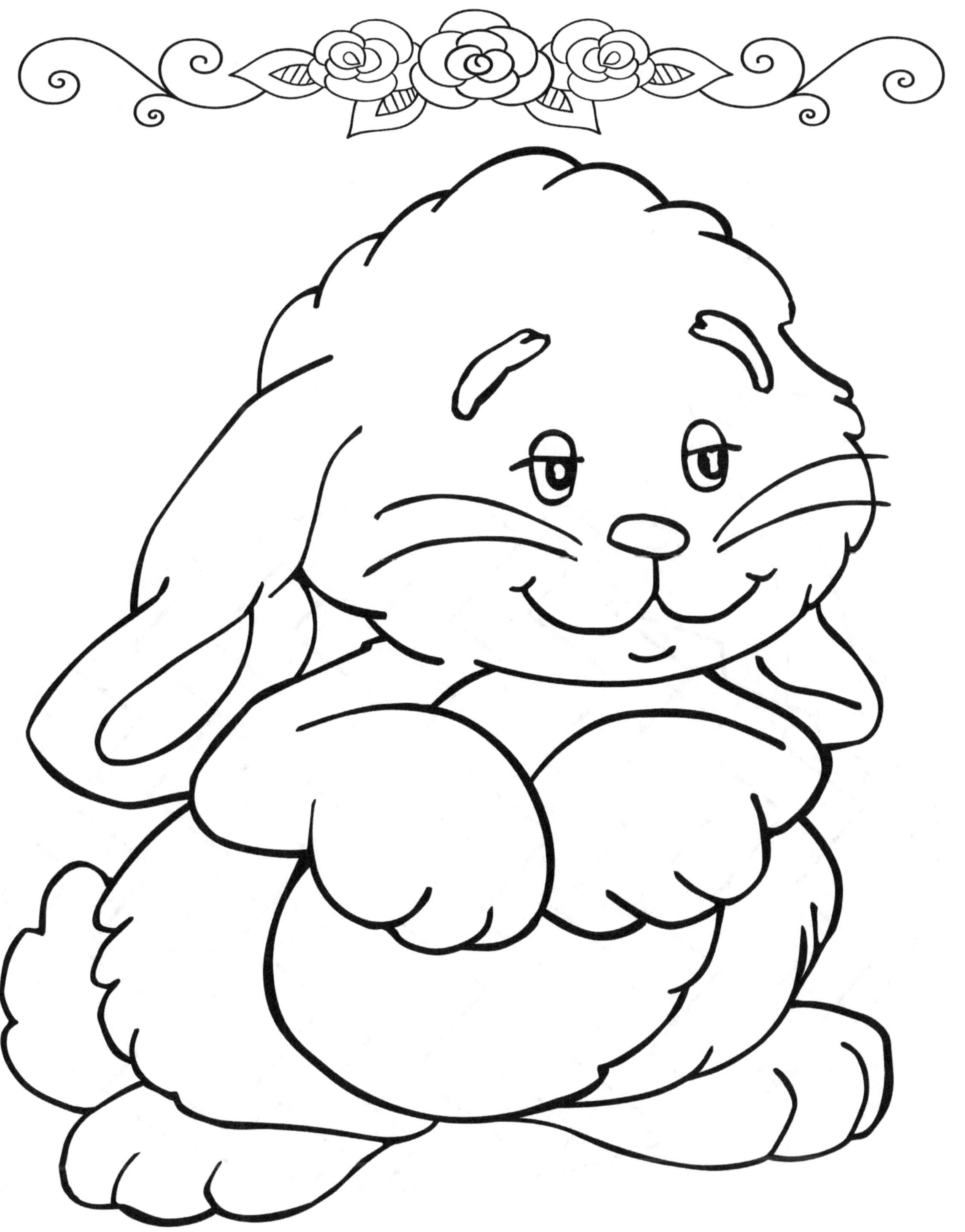

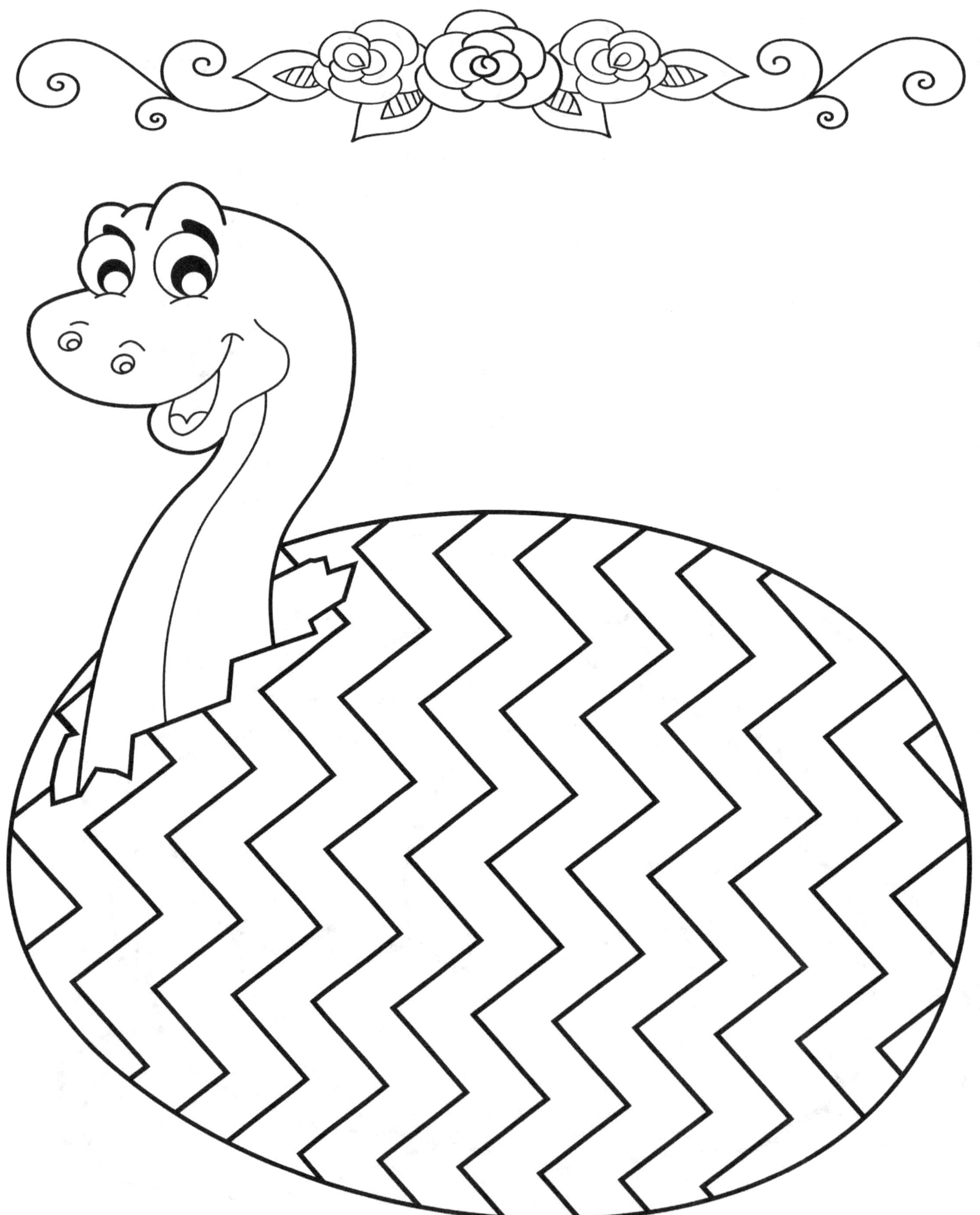

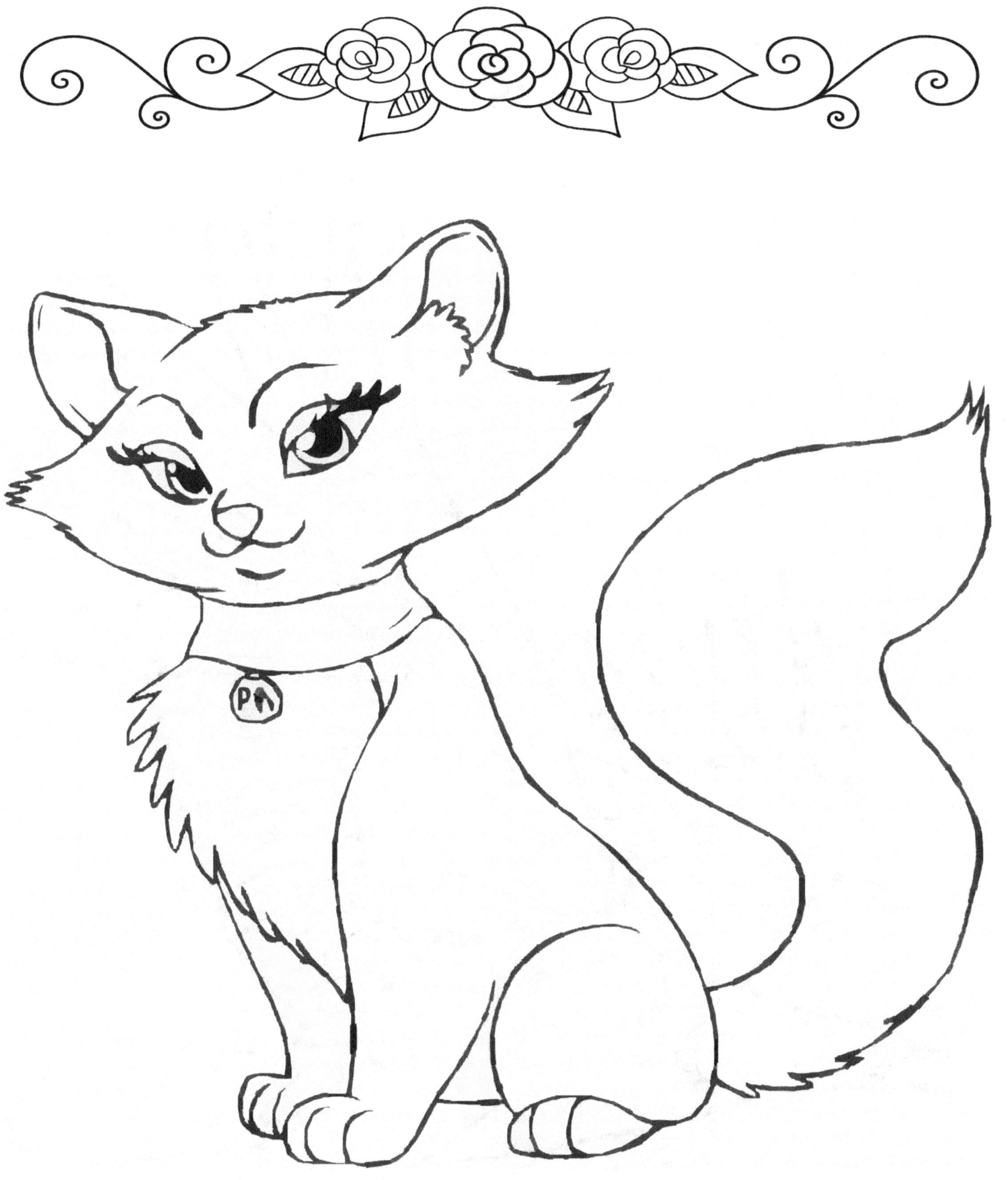

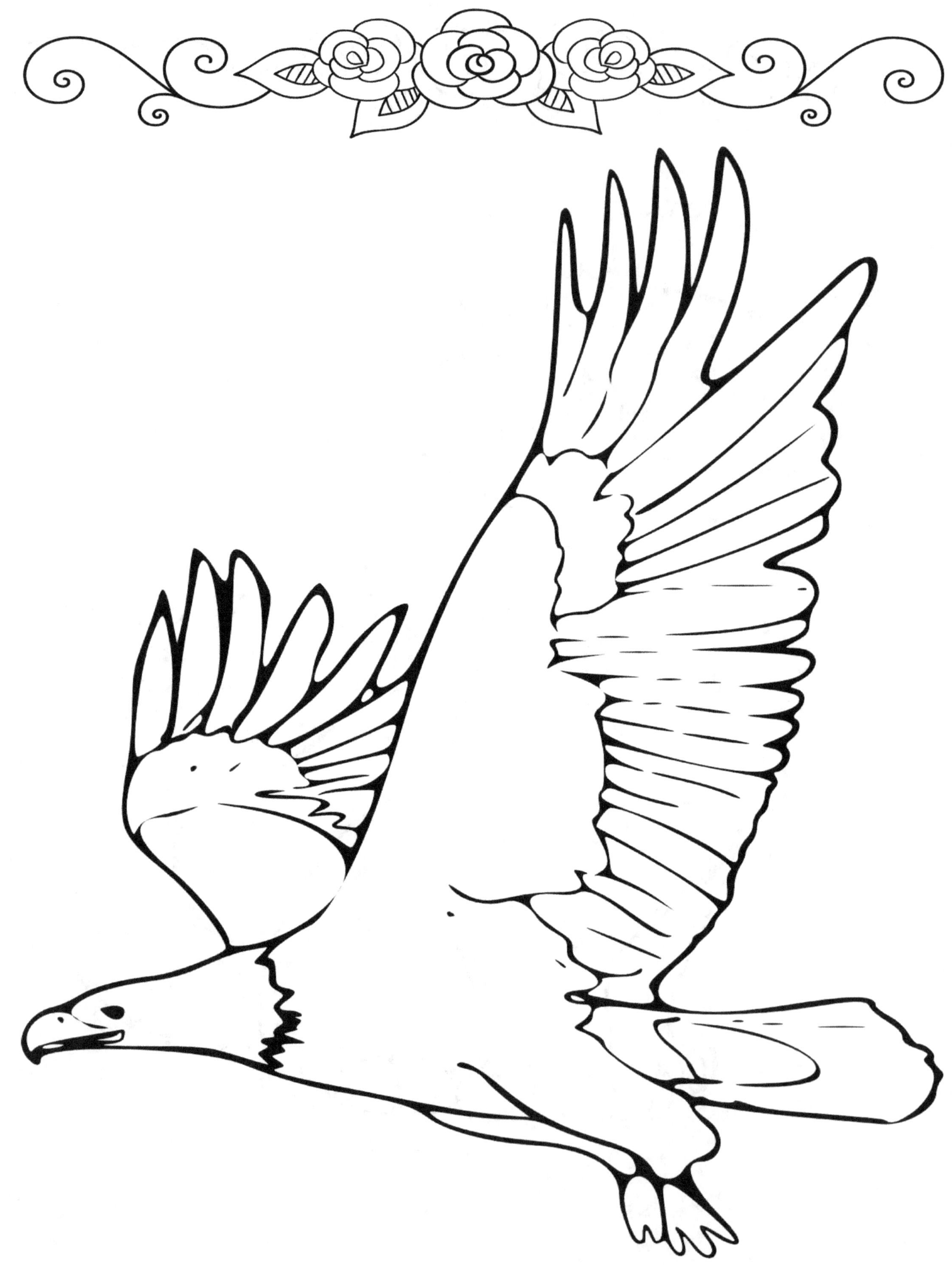

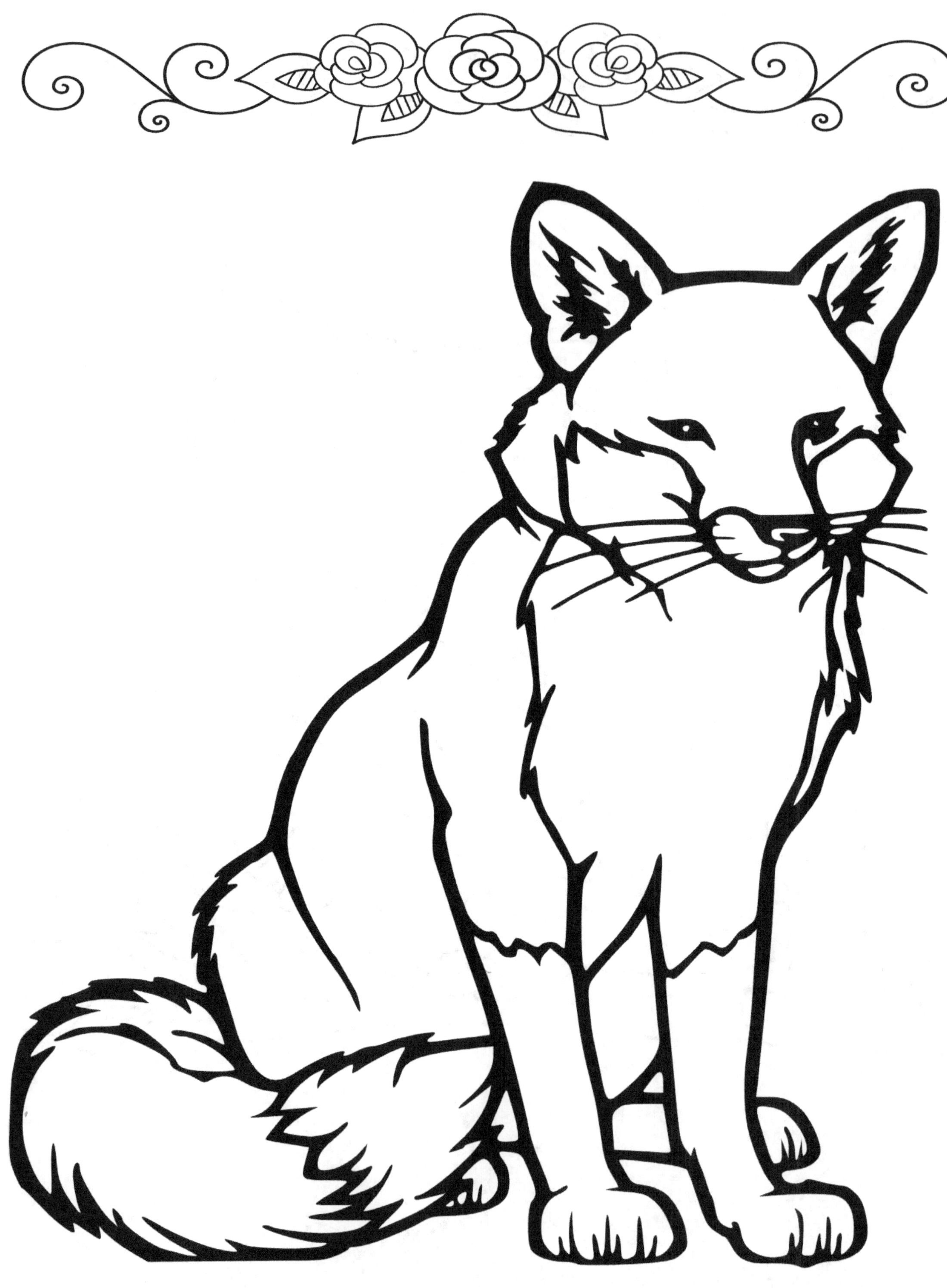

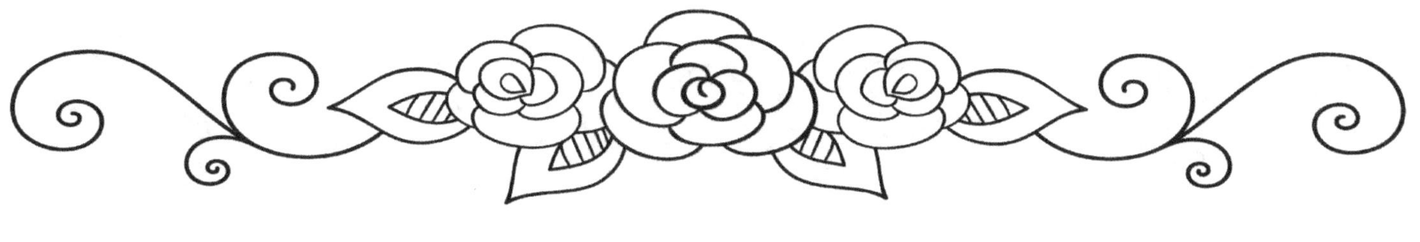

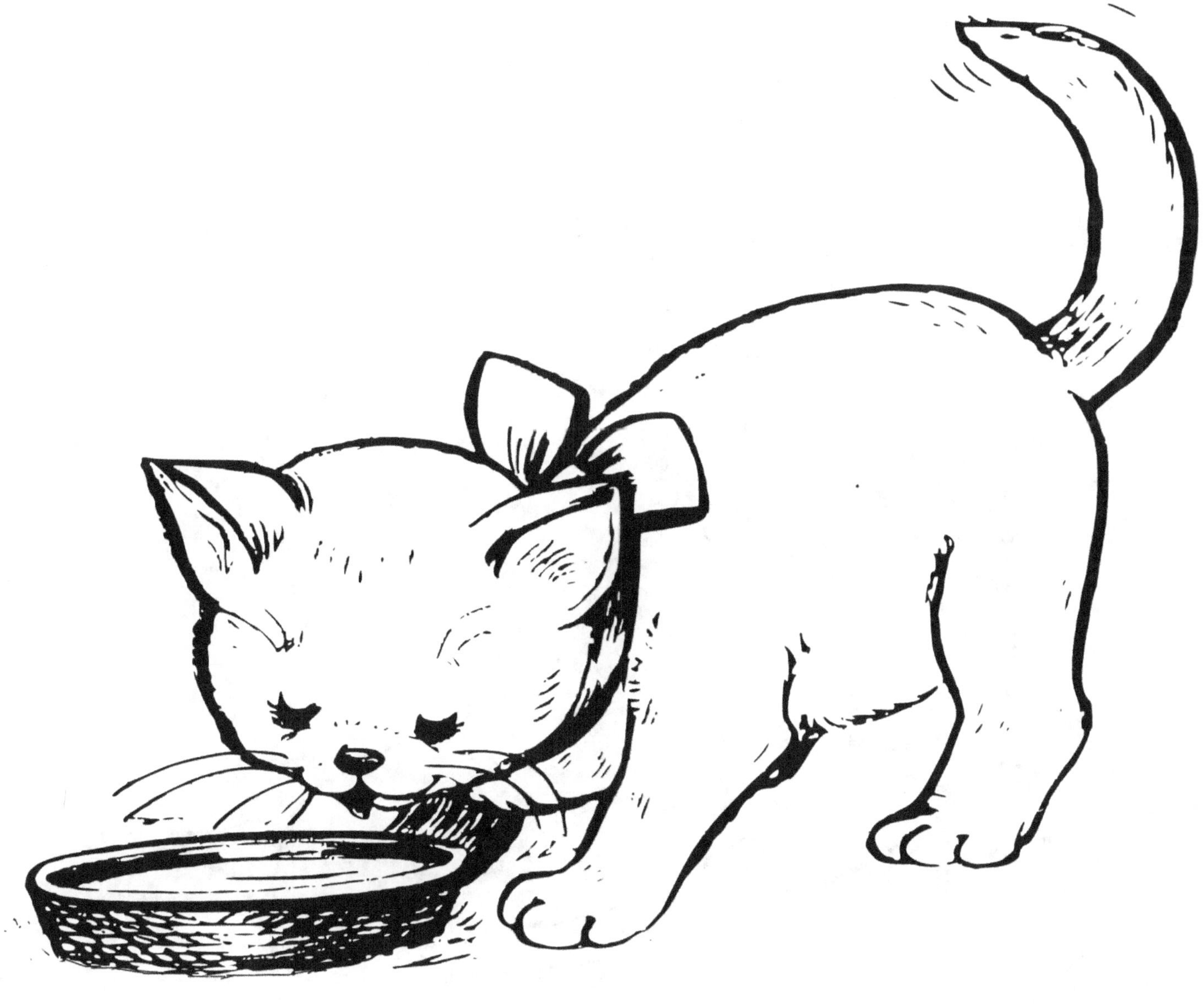

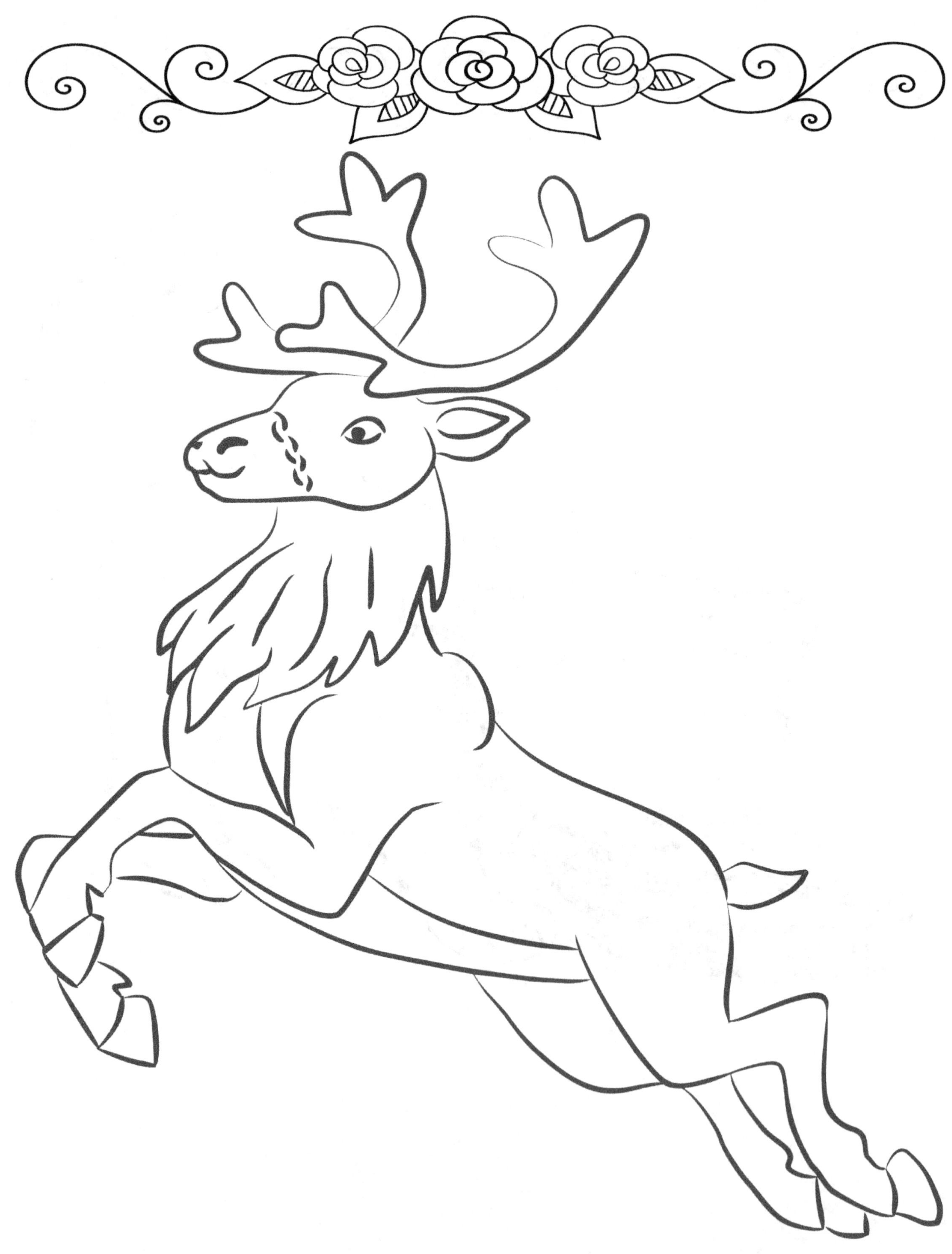

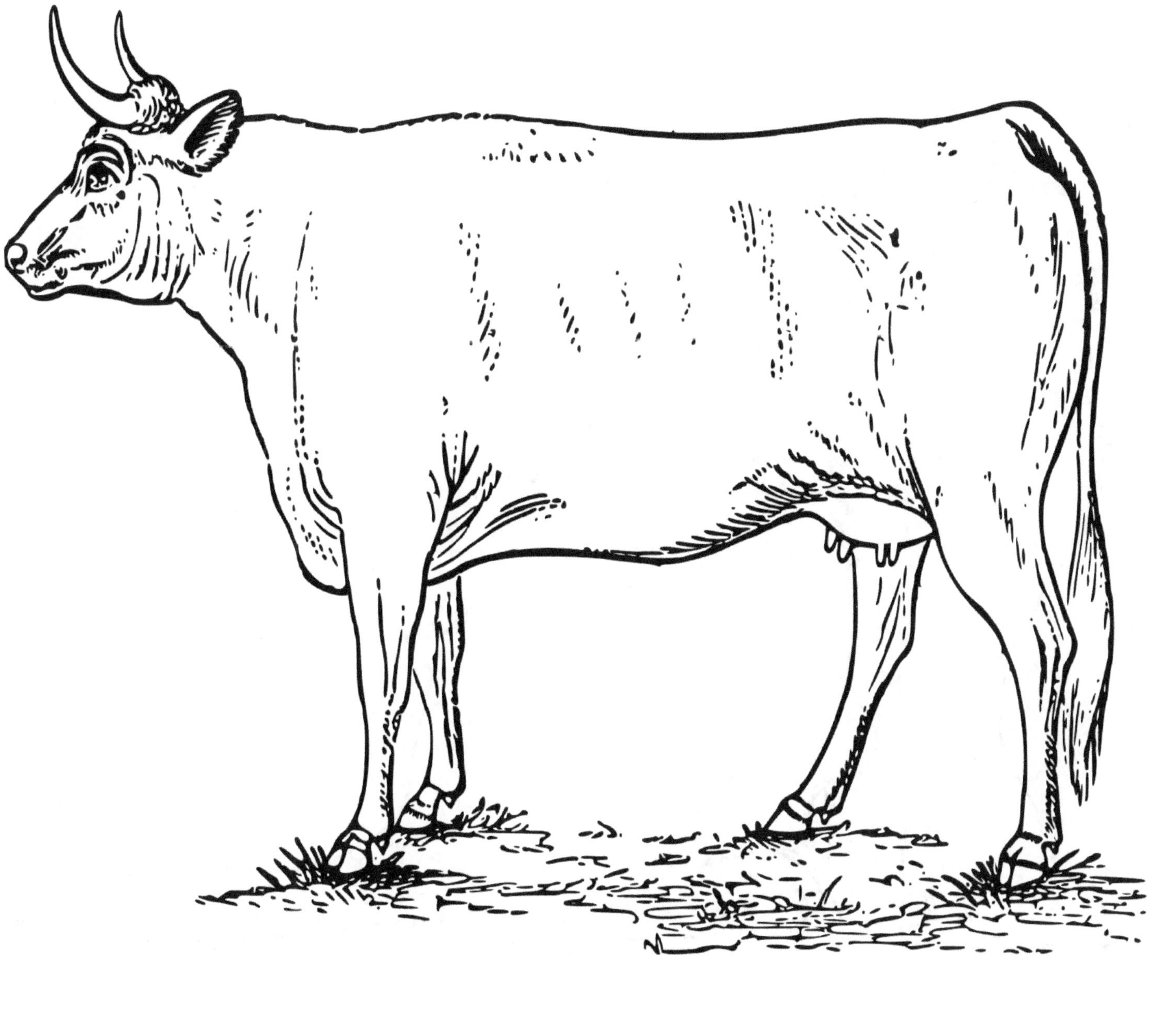

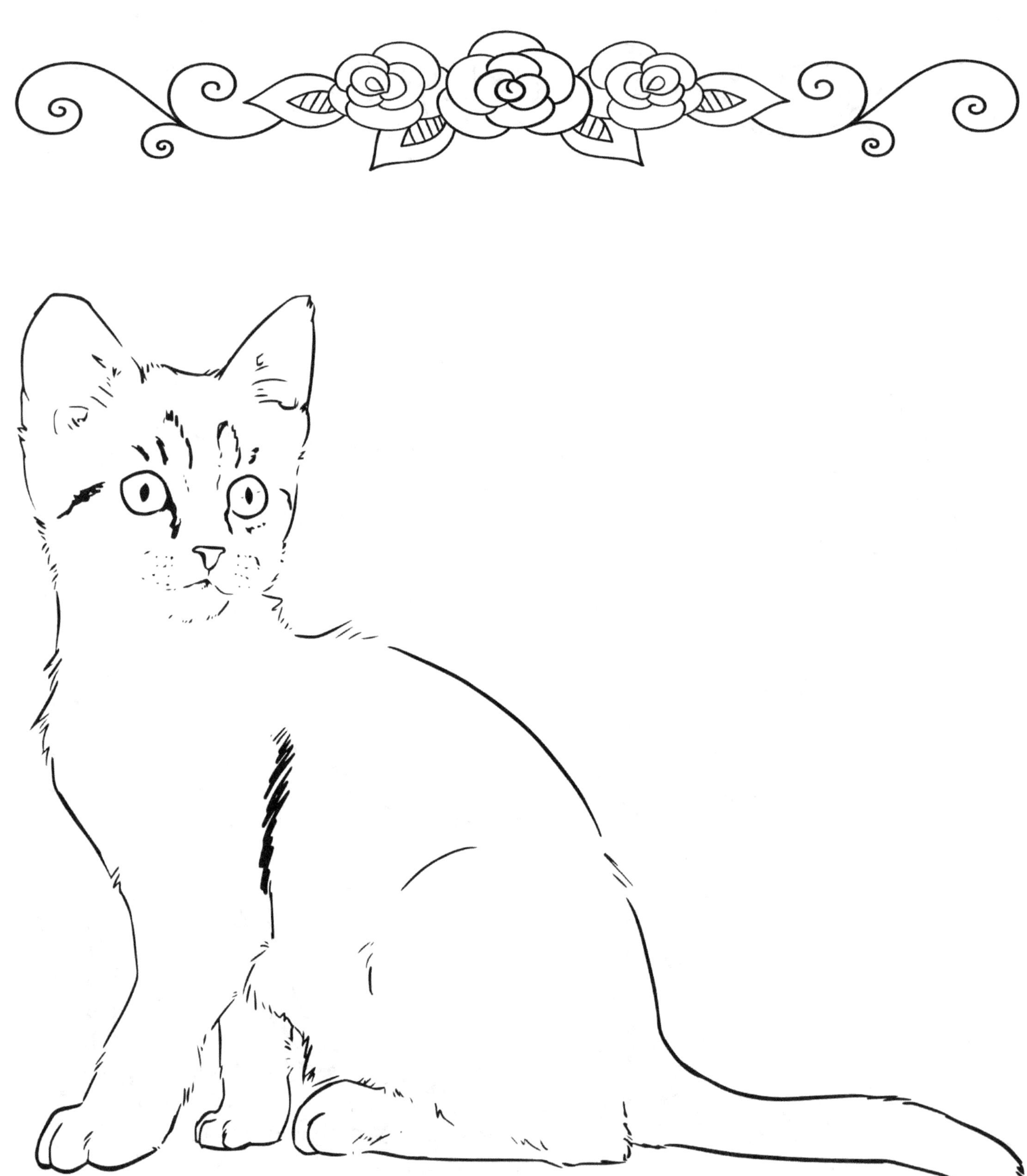

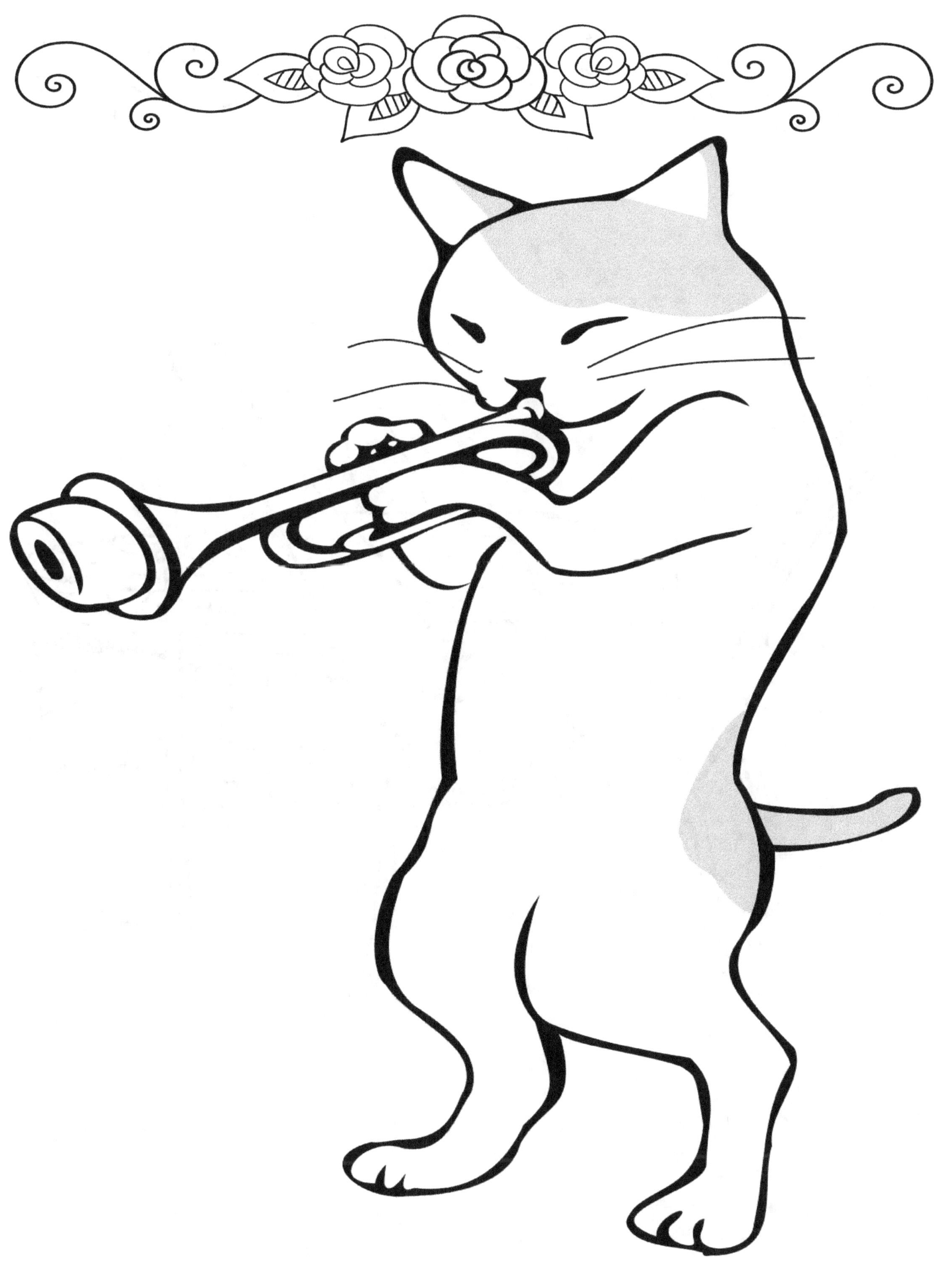

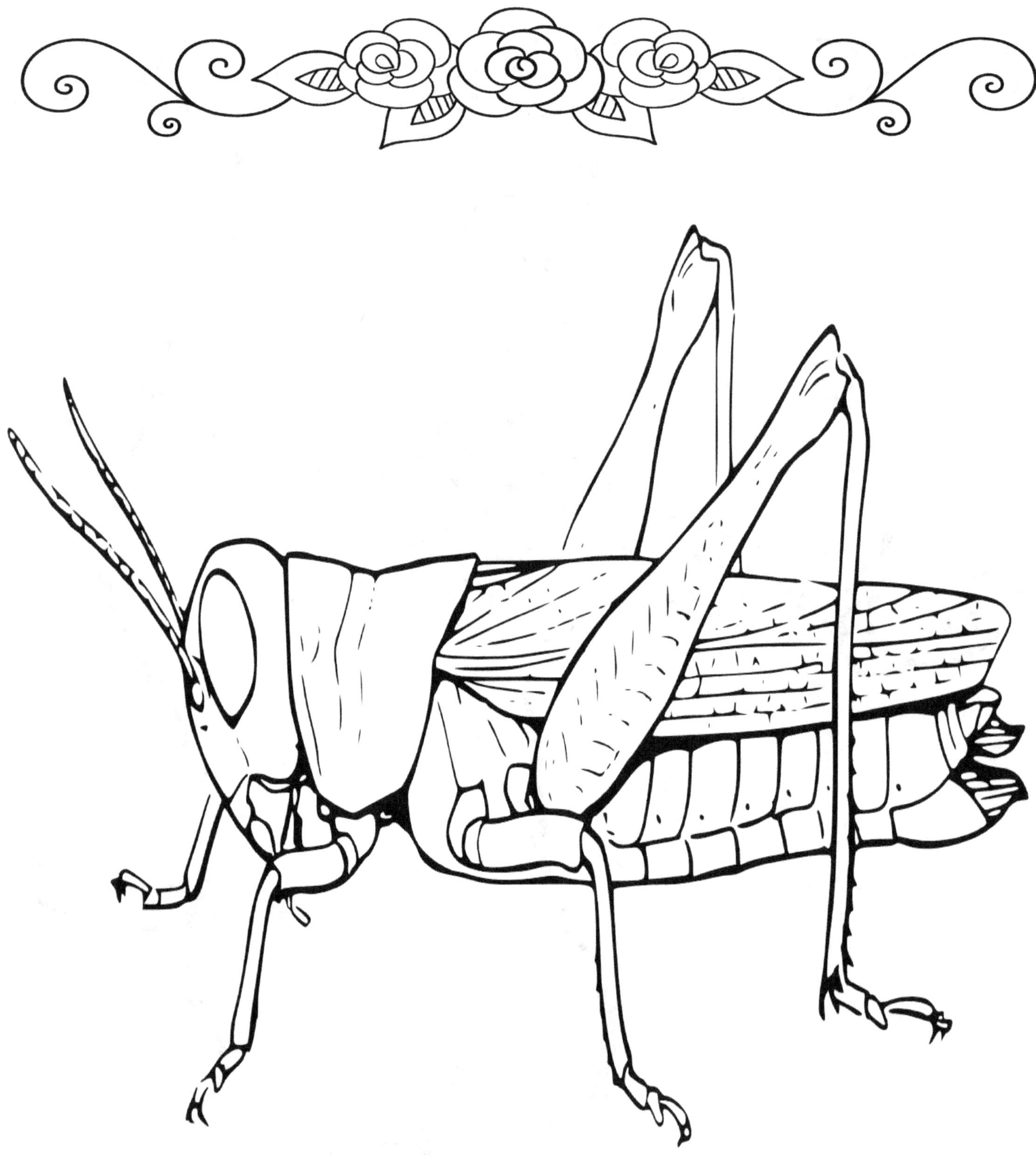

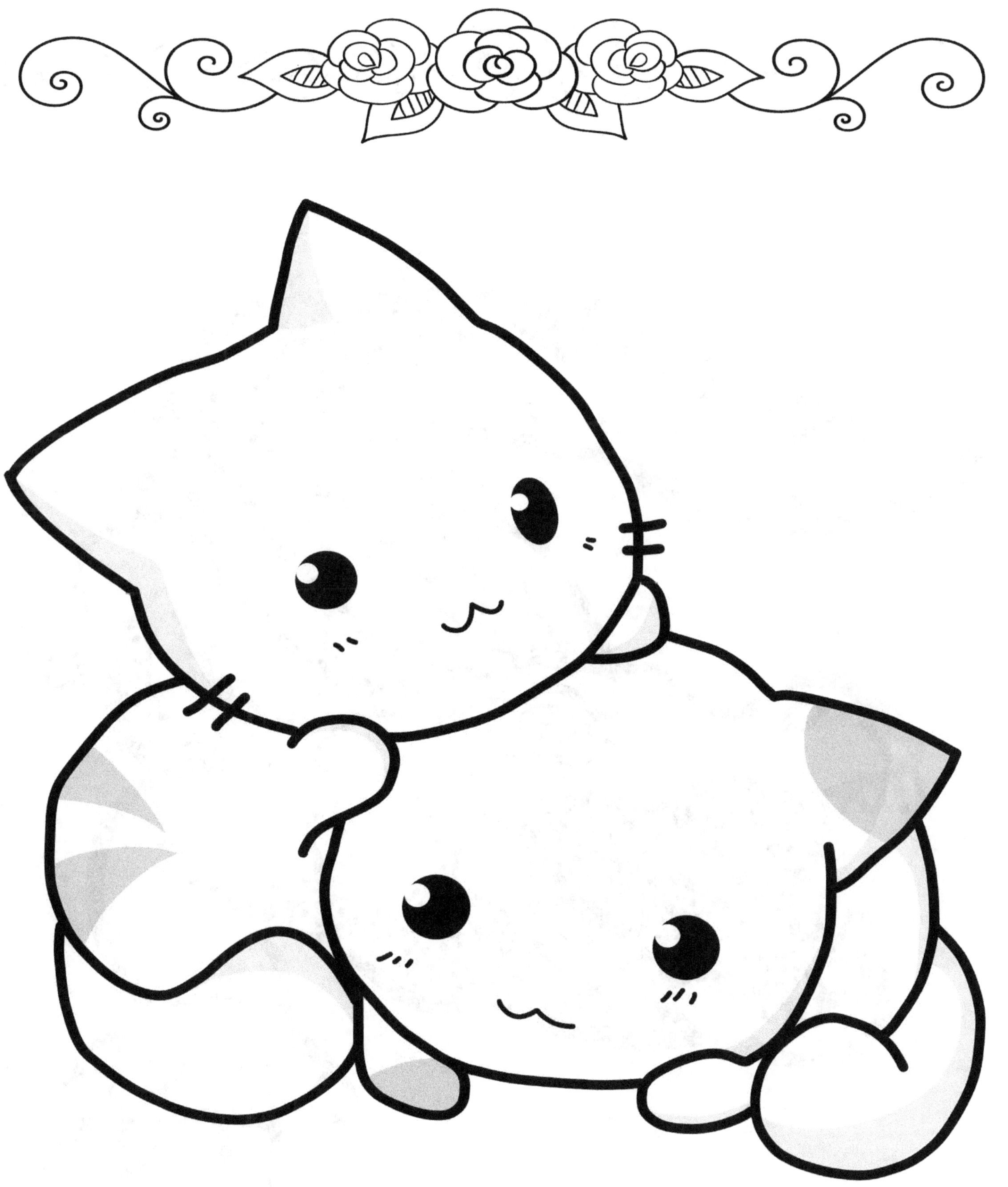

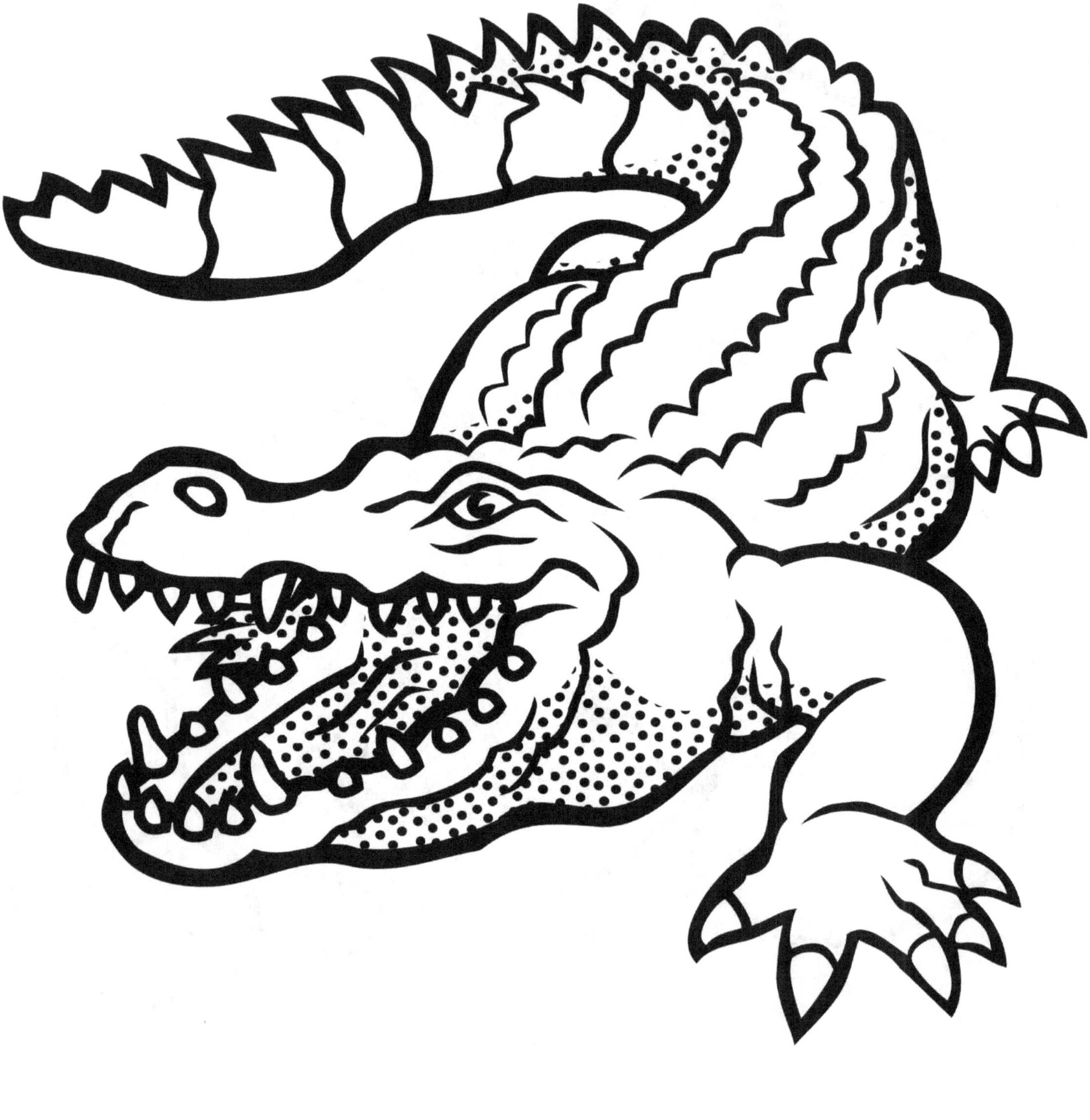

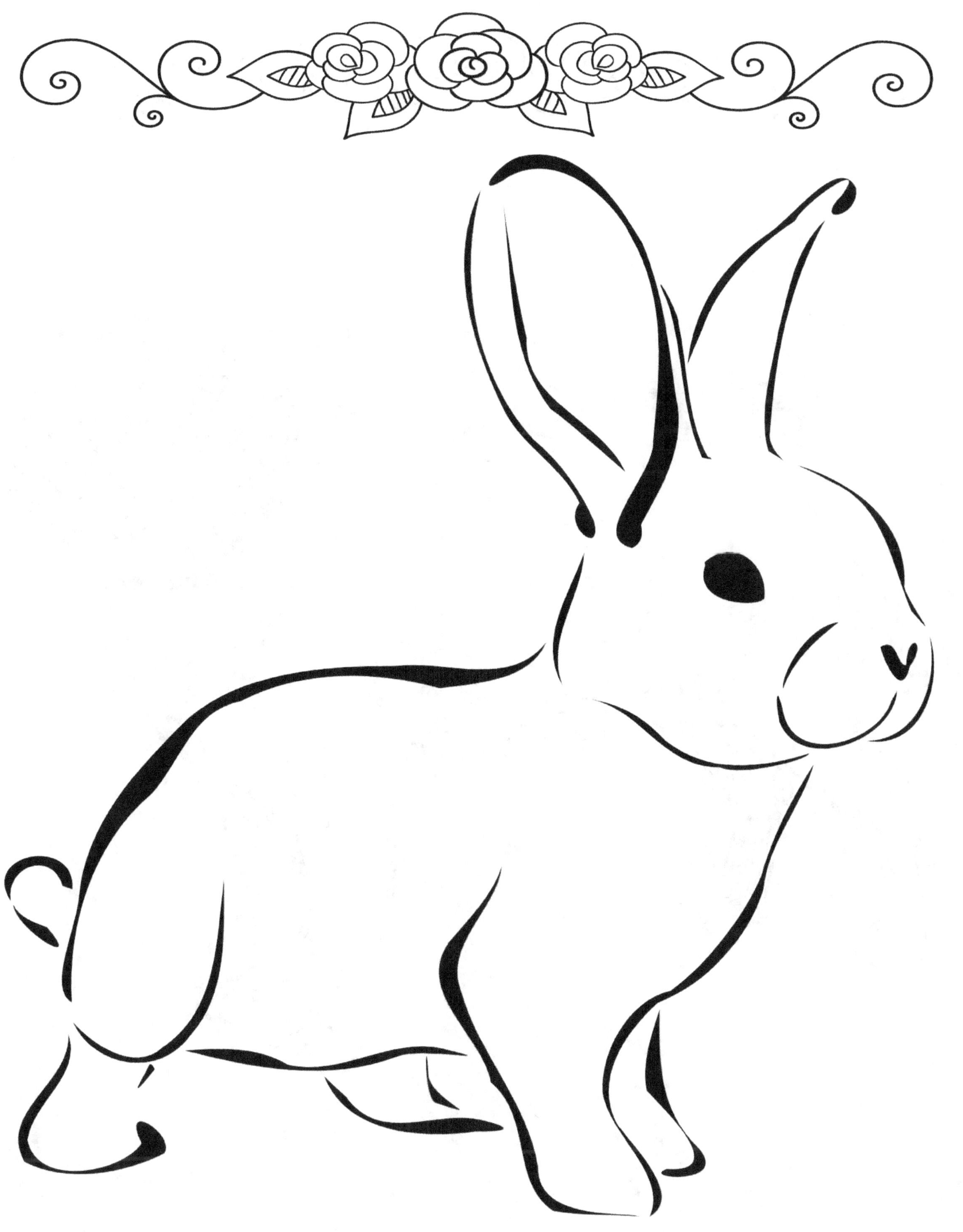

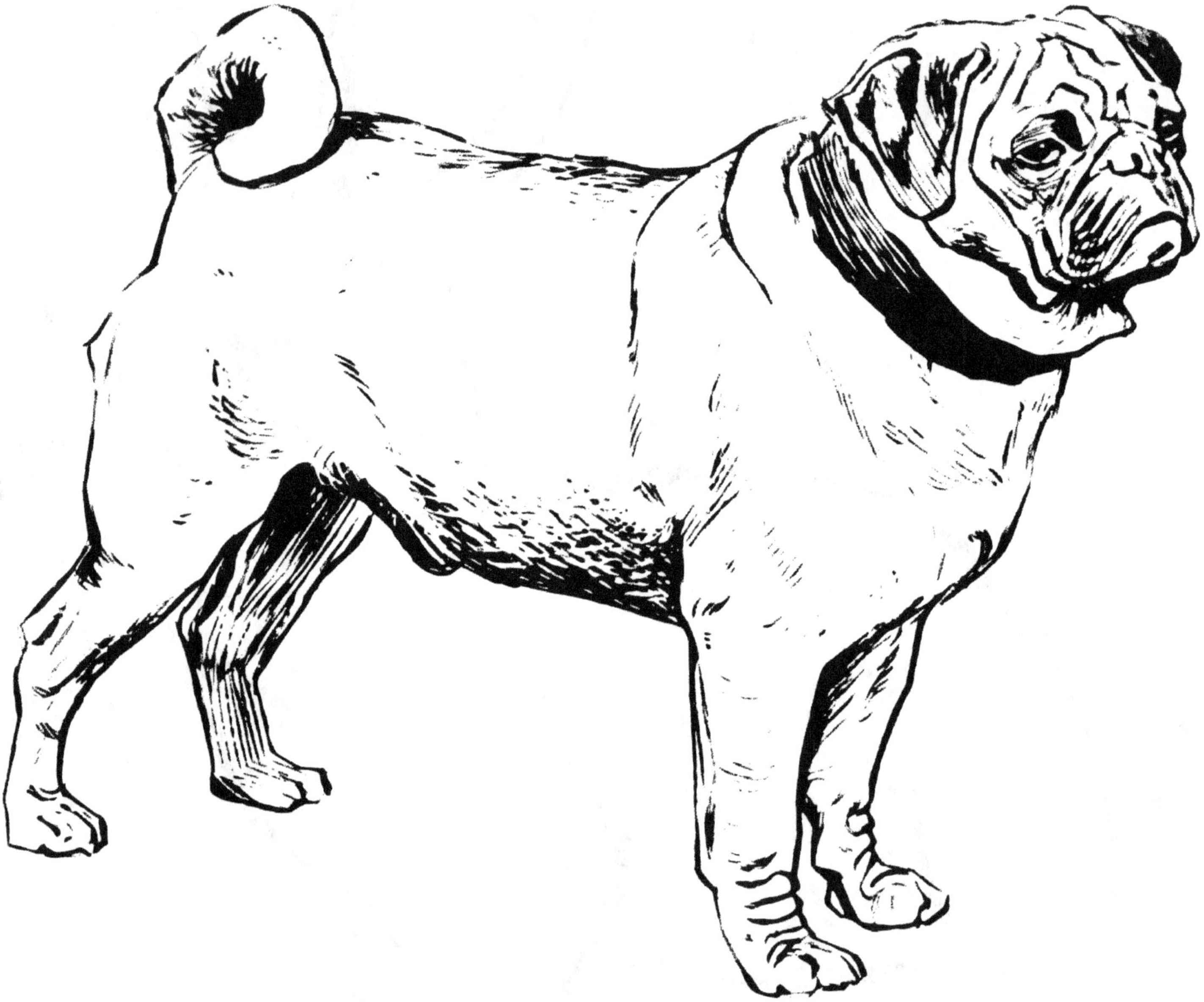

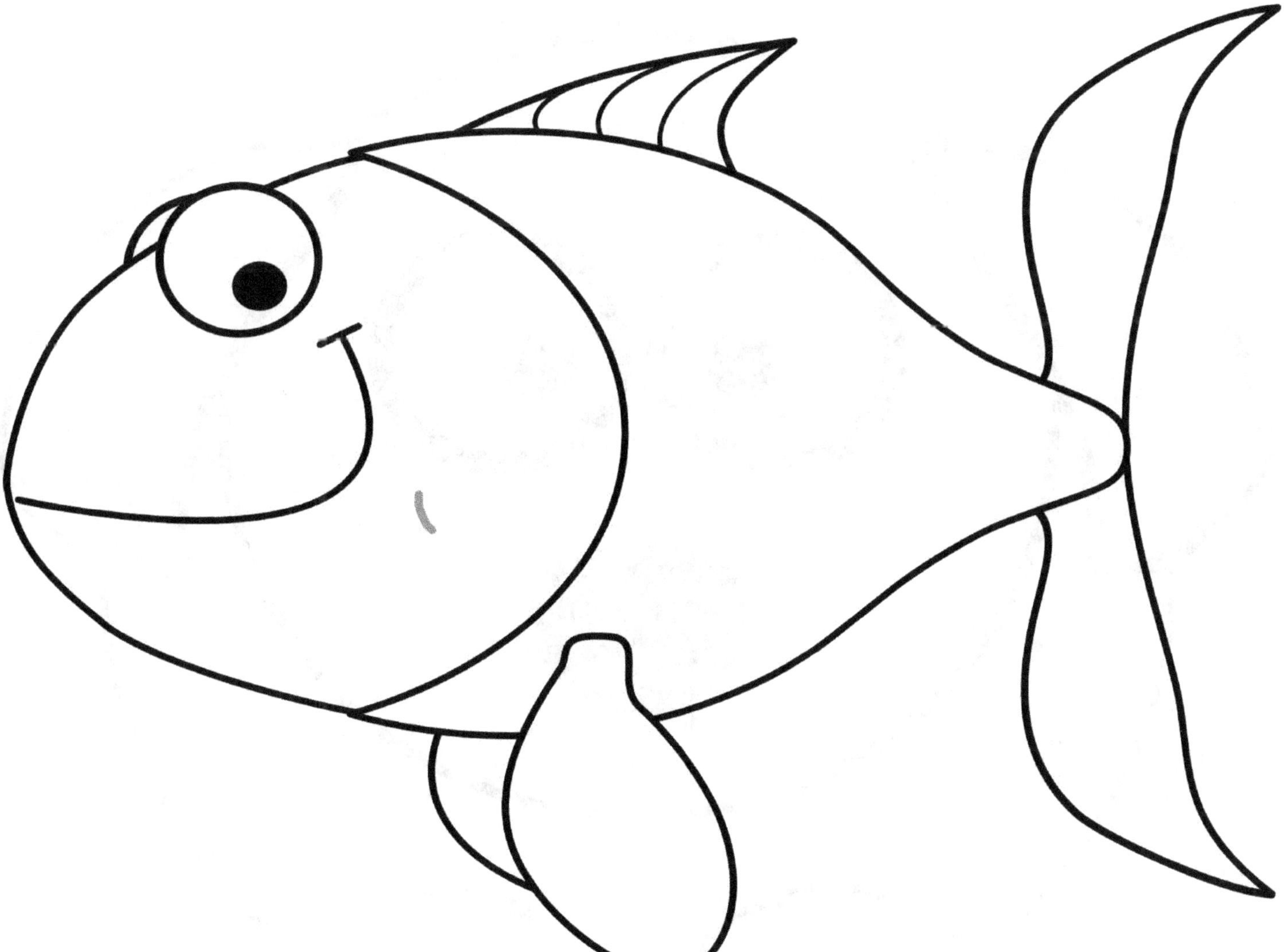

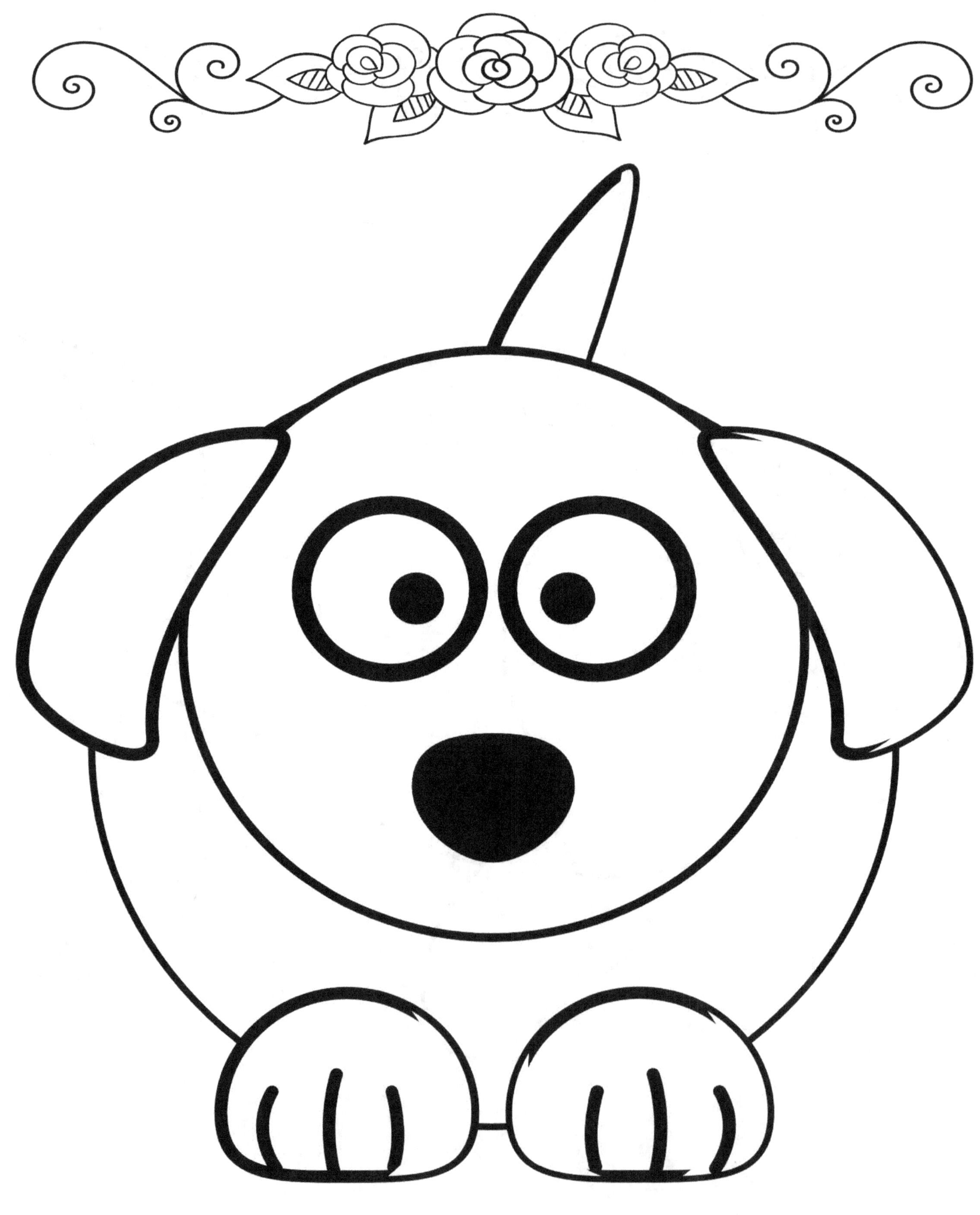

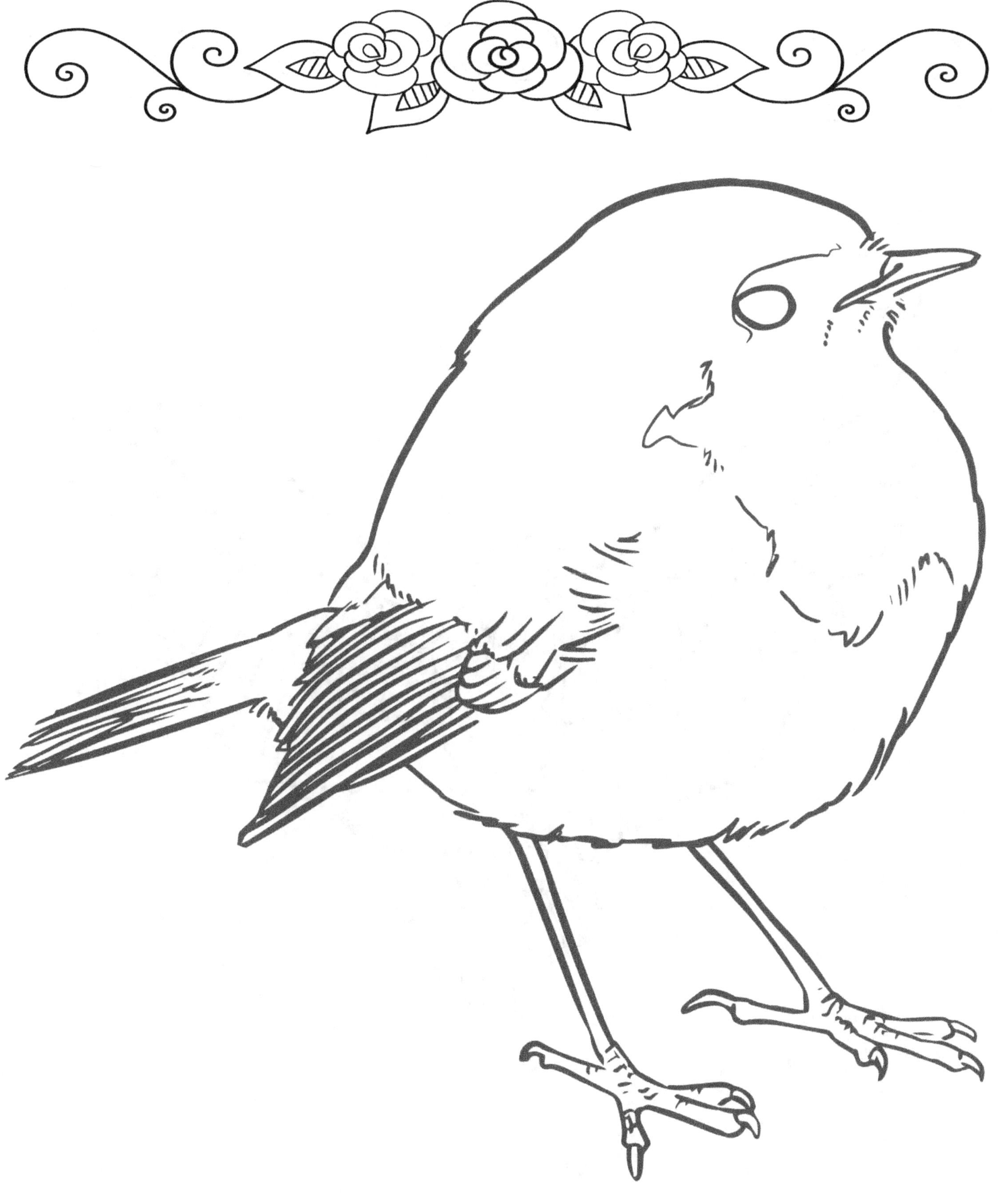

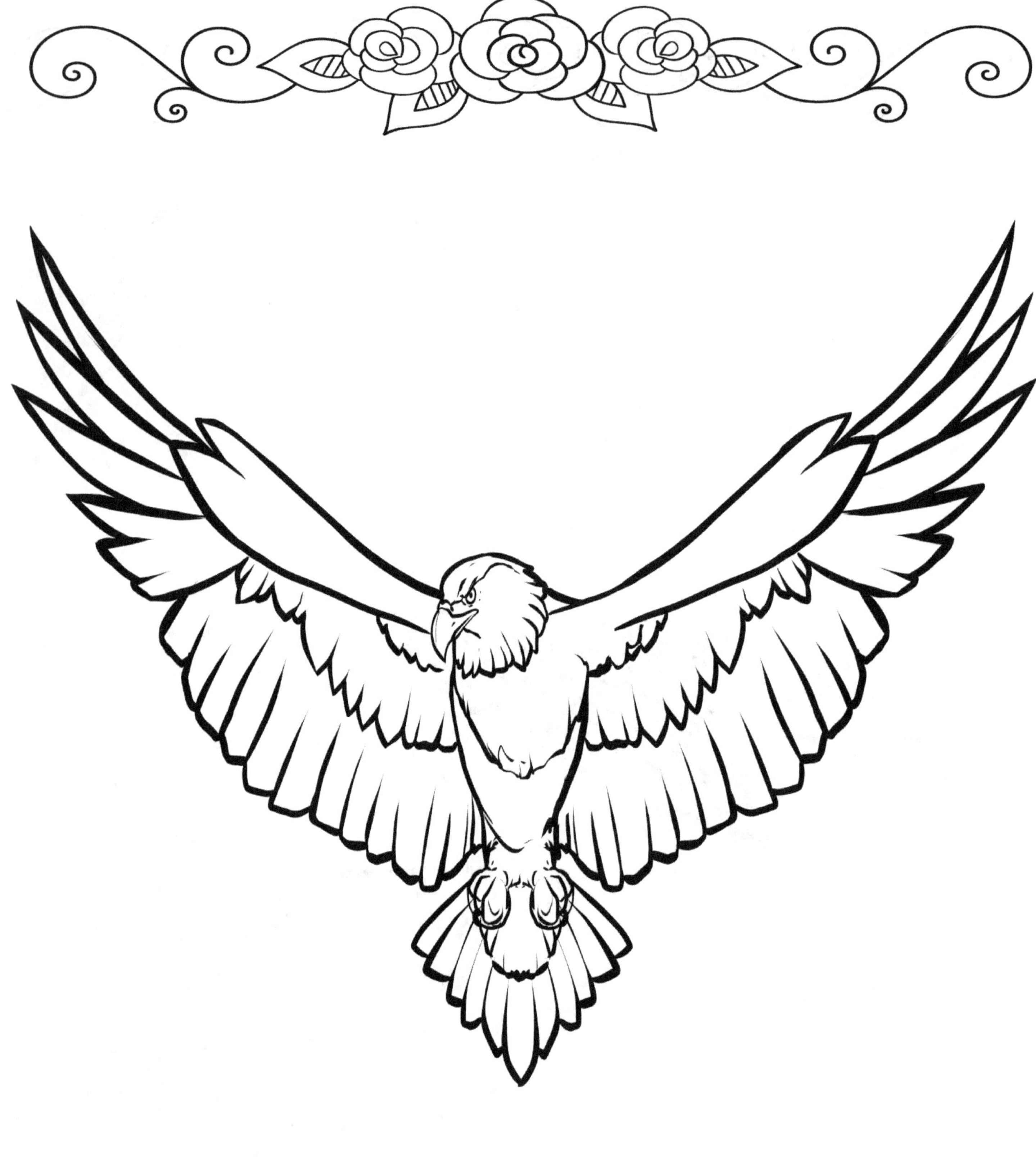

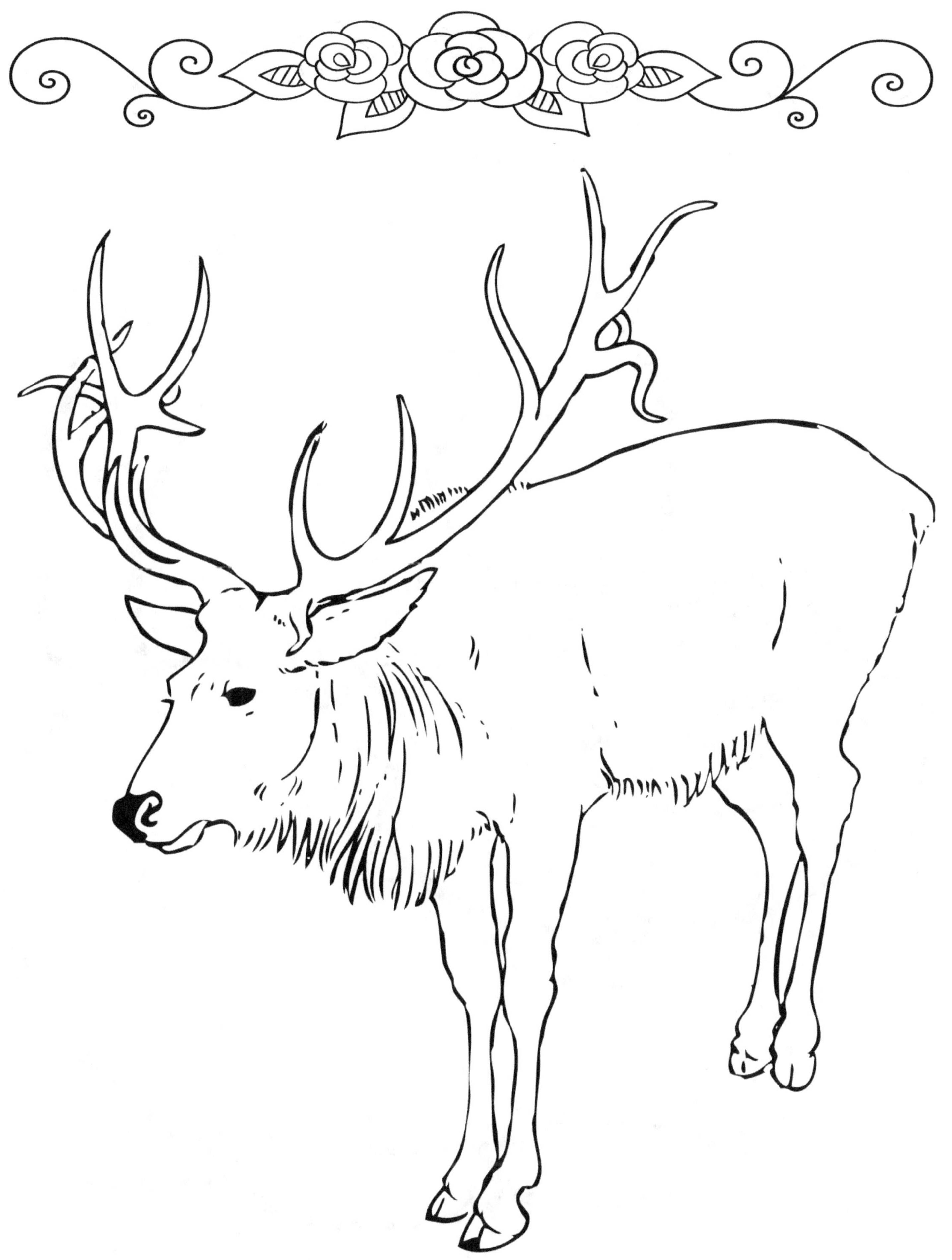

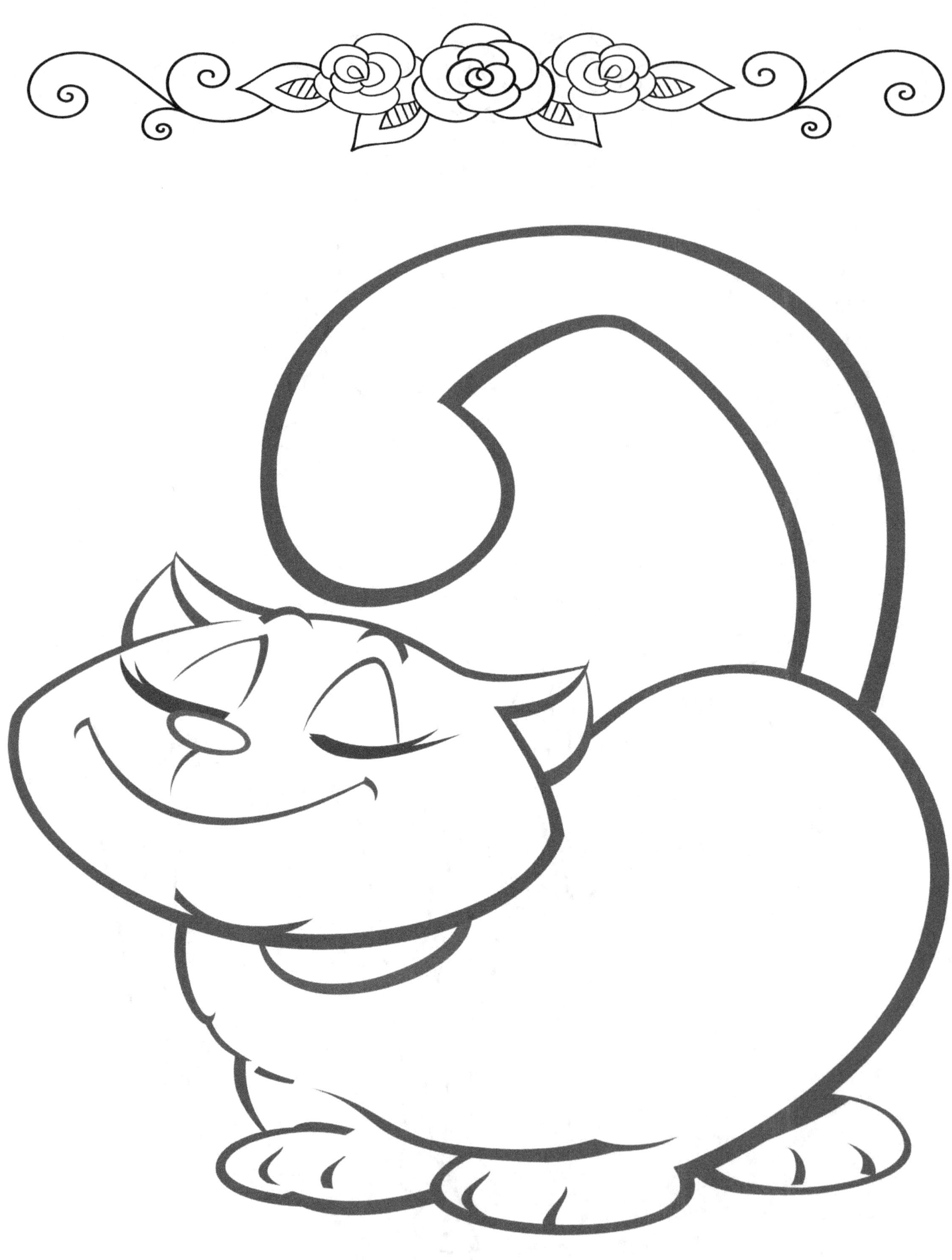

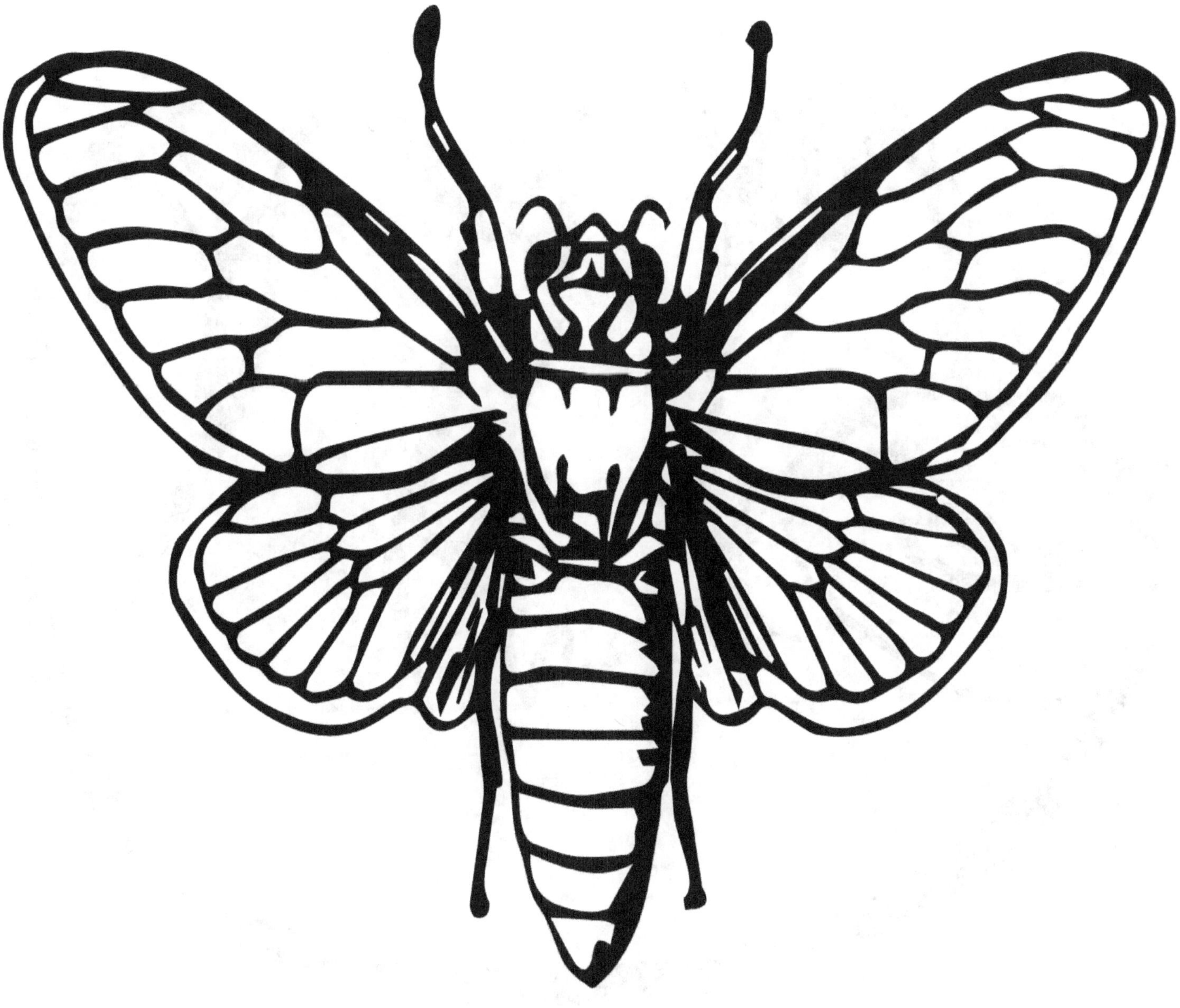

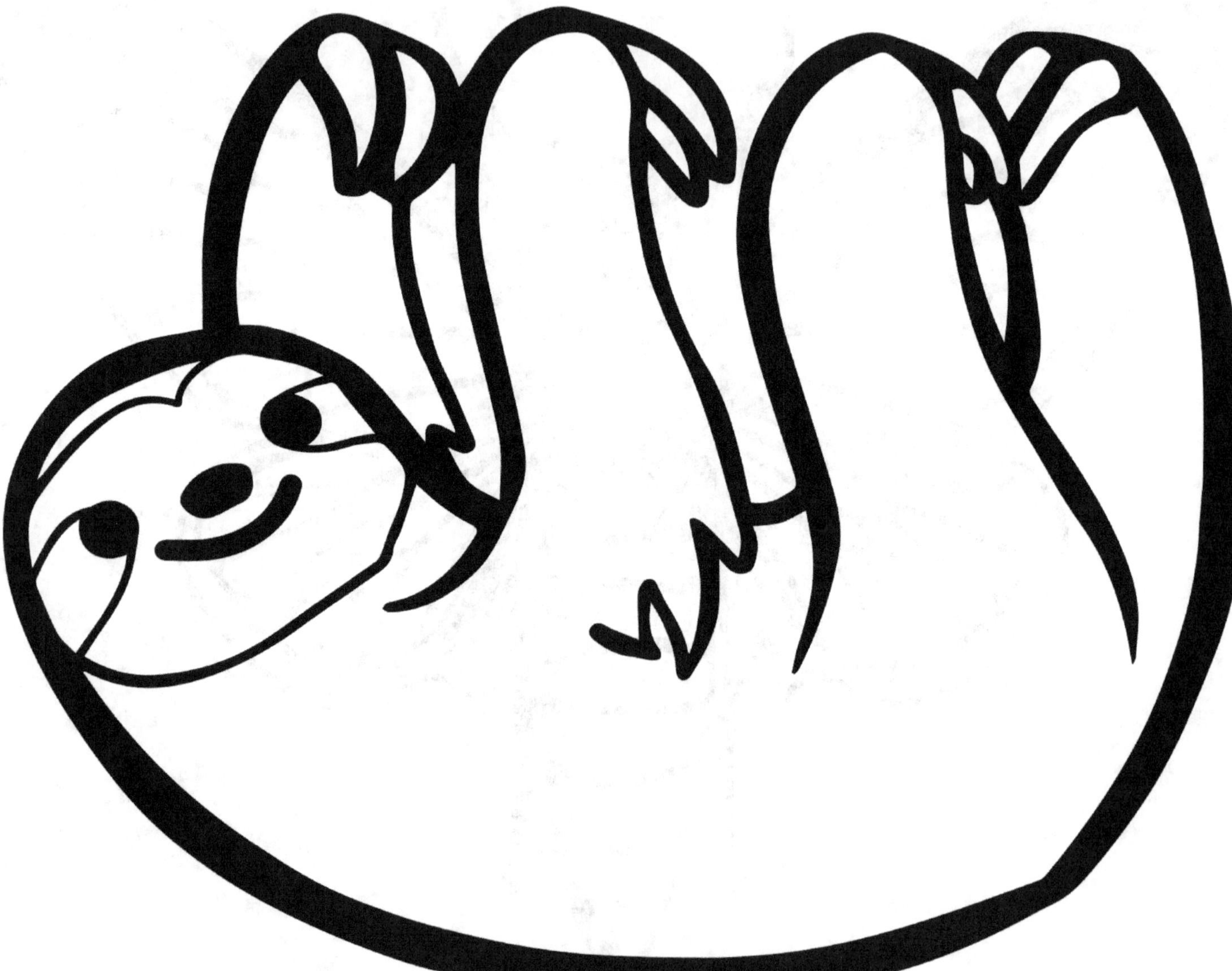

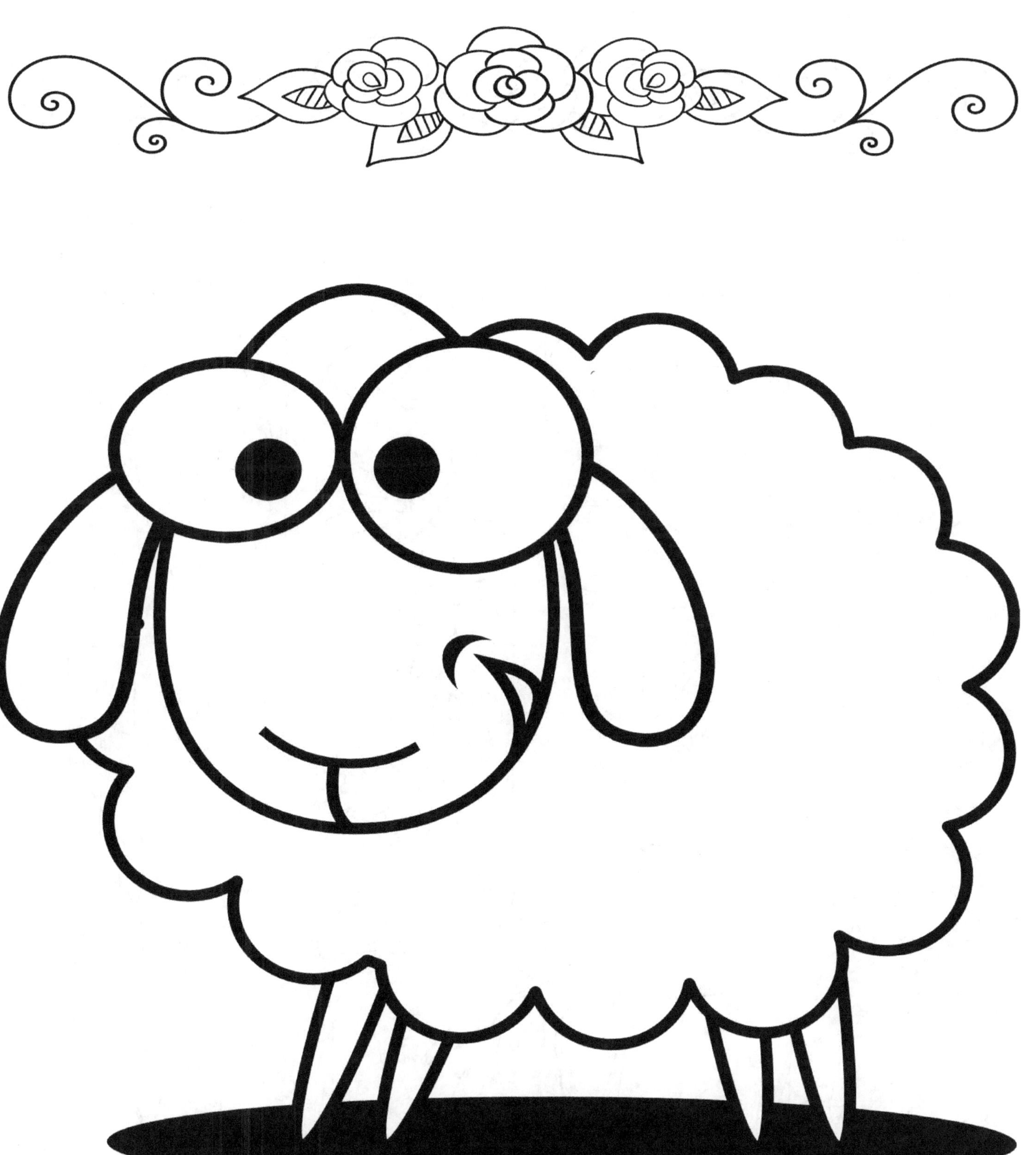

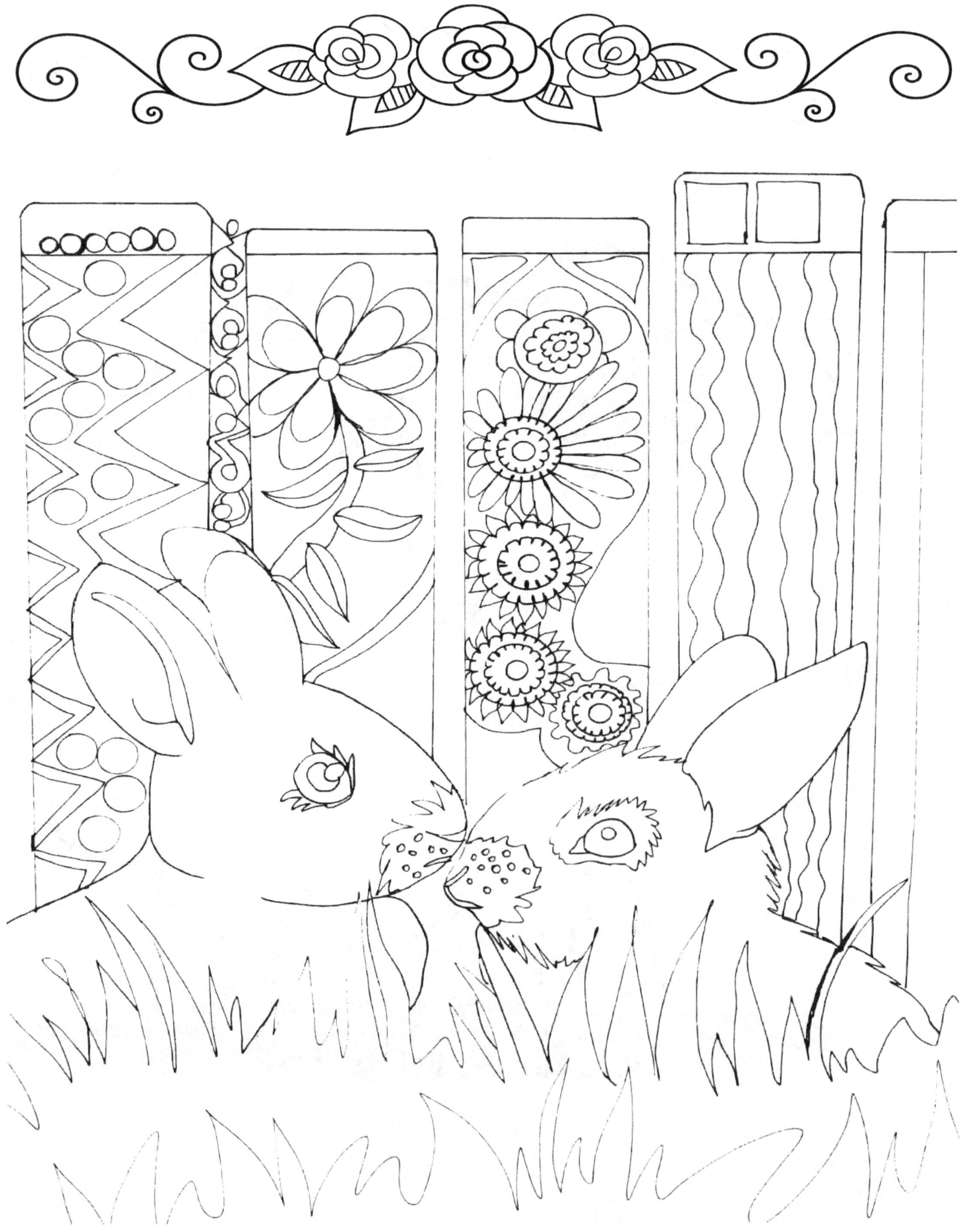

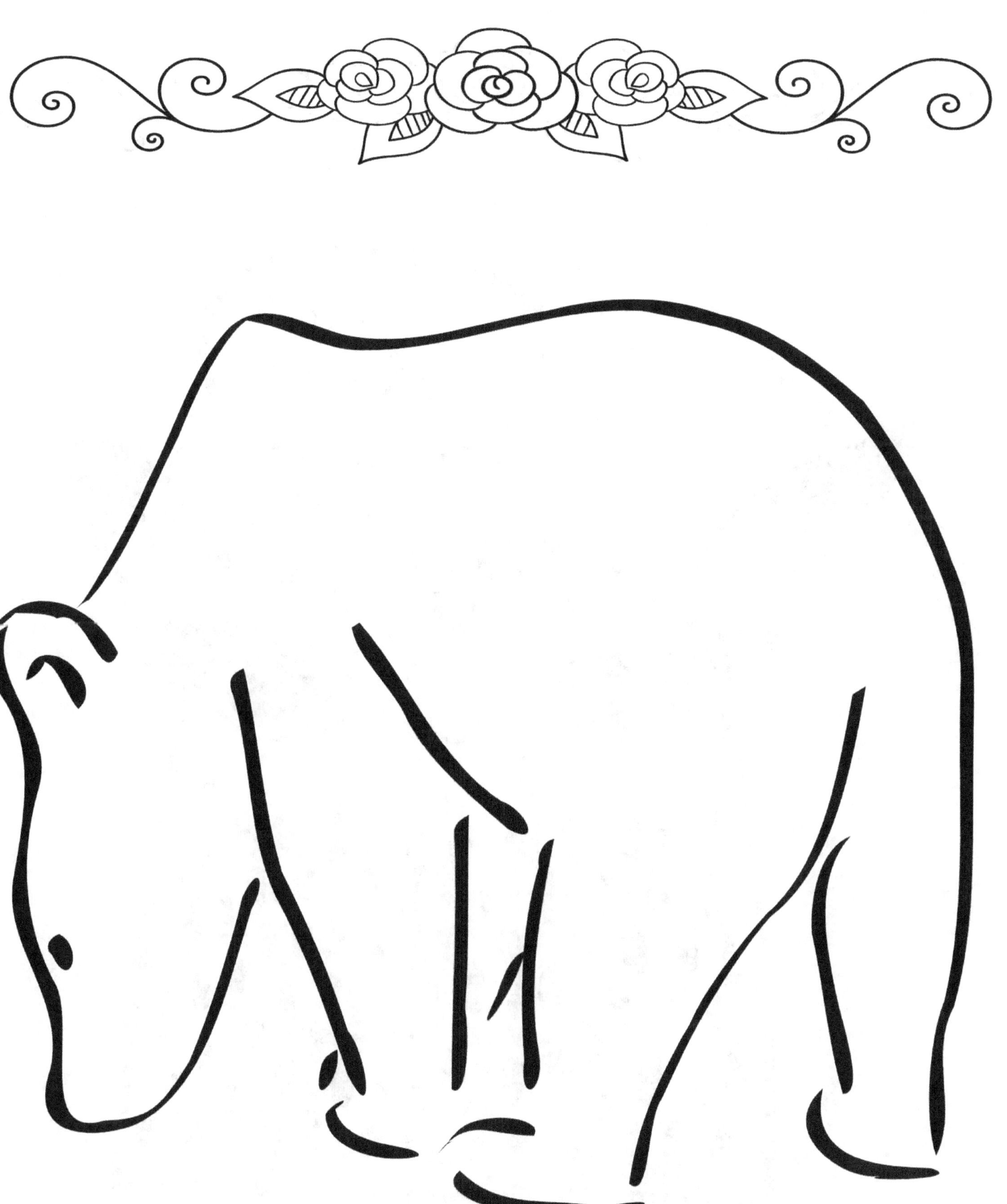

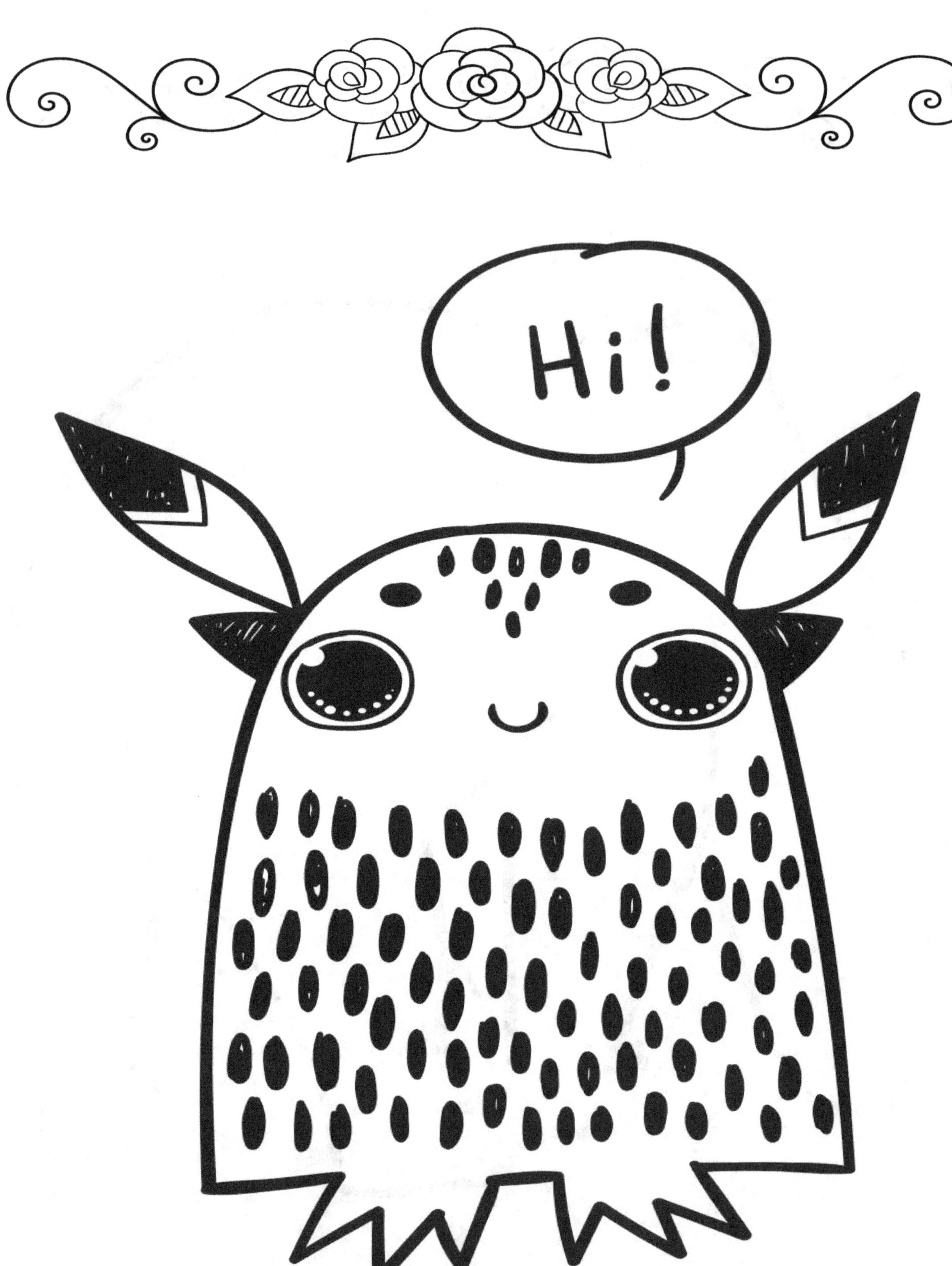
Hi!

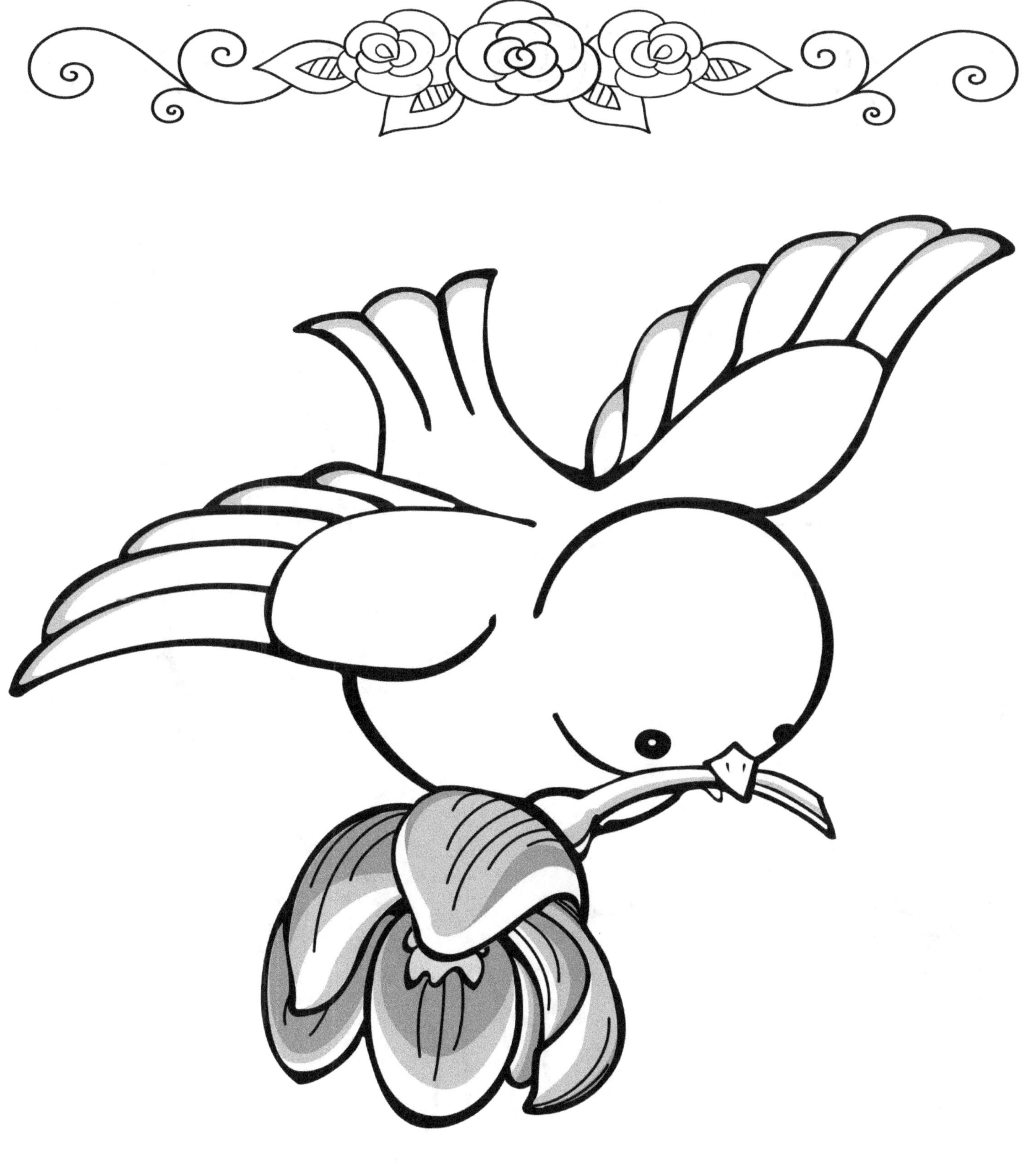

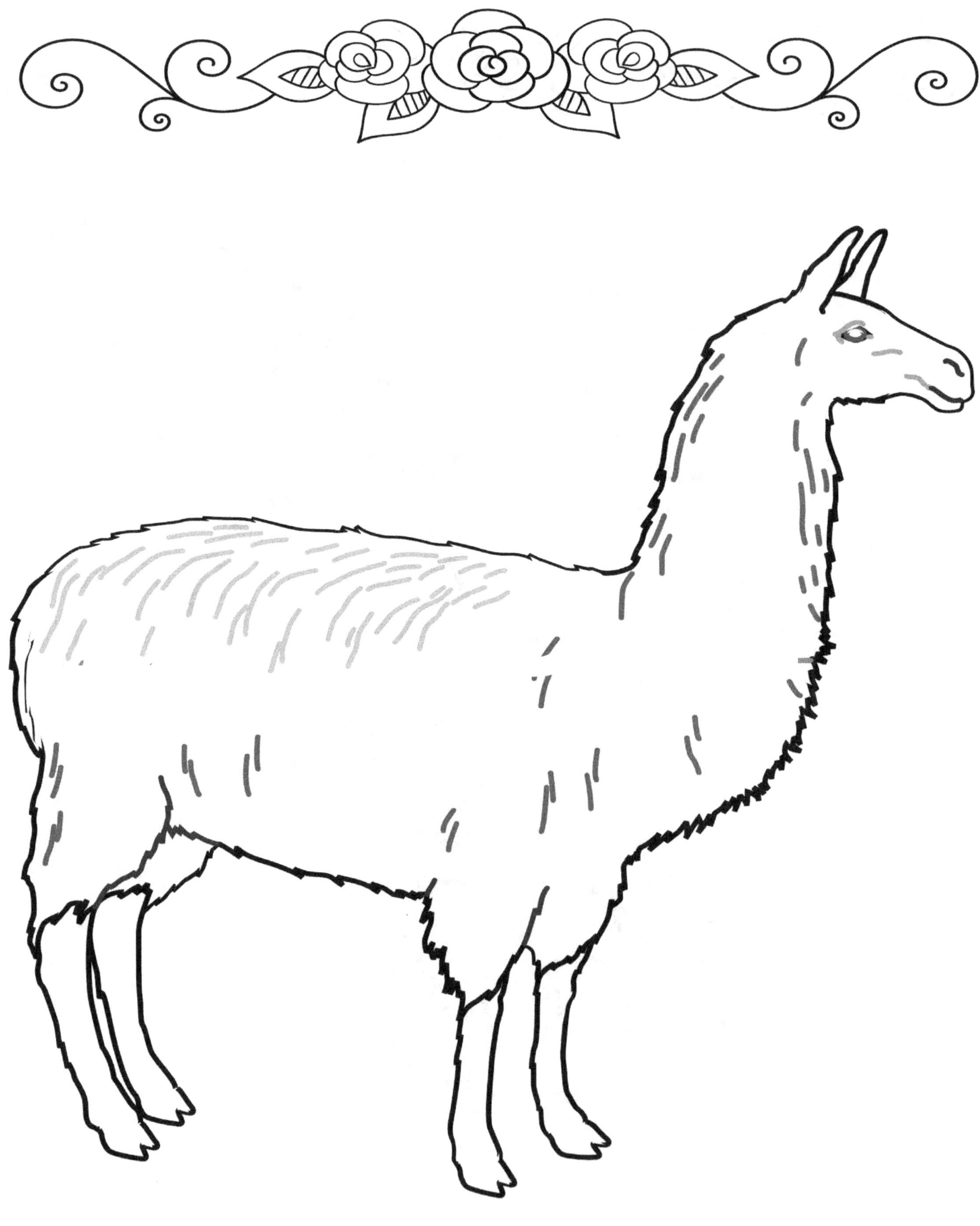

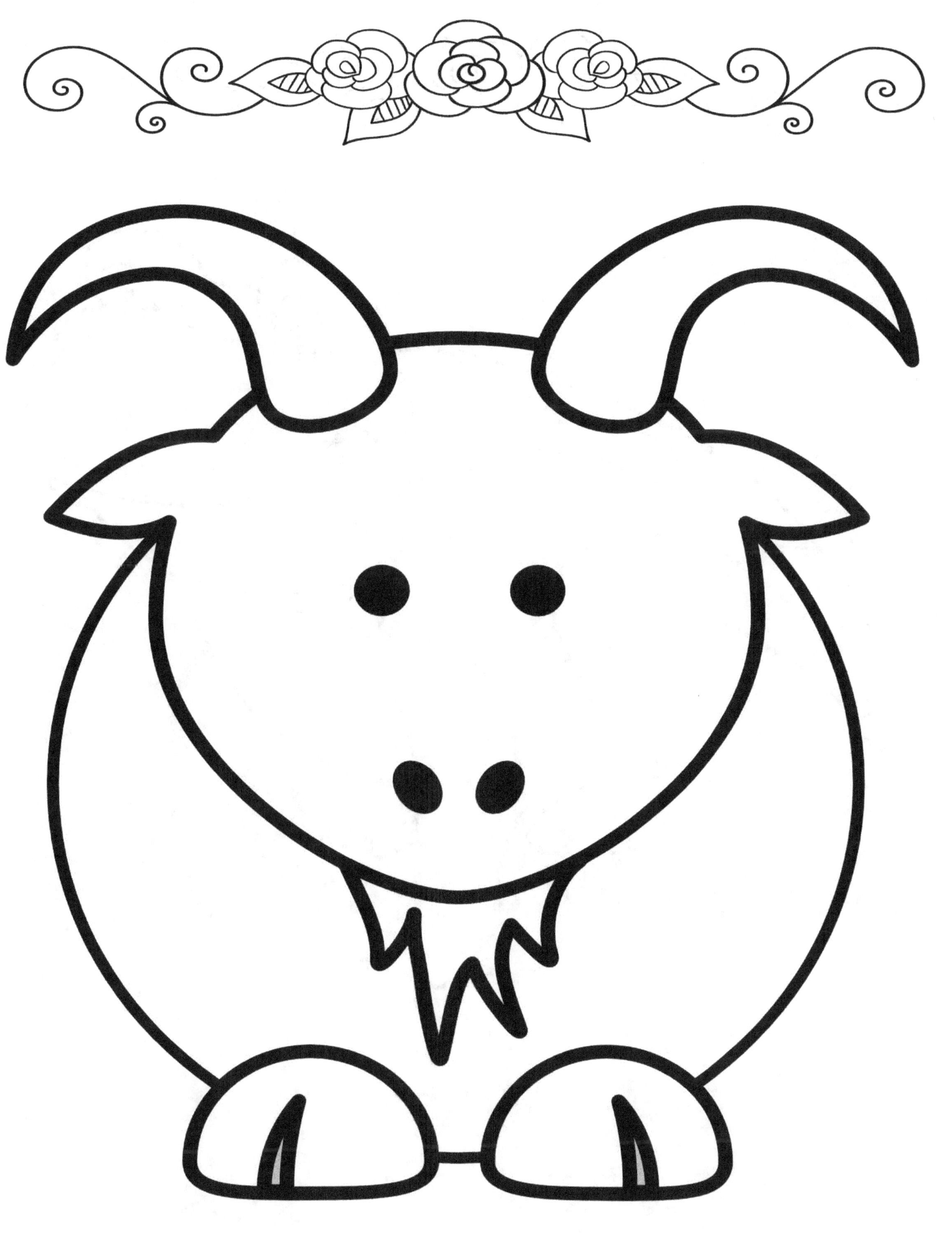

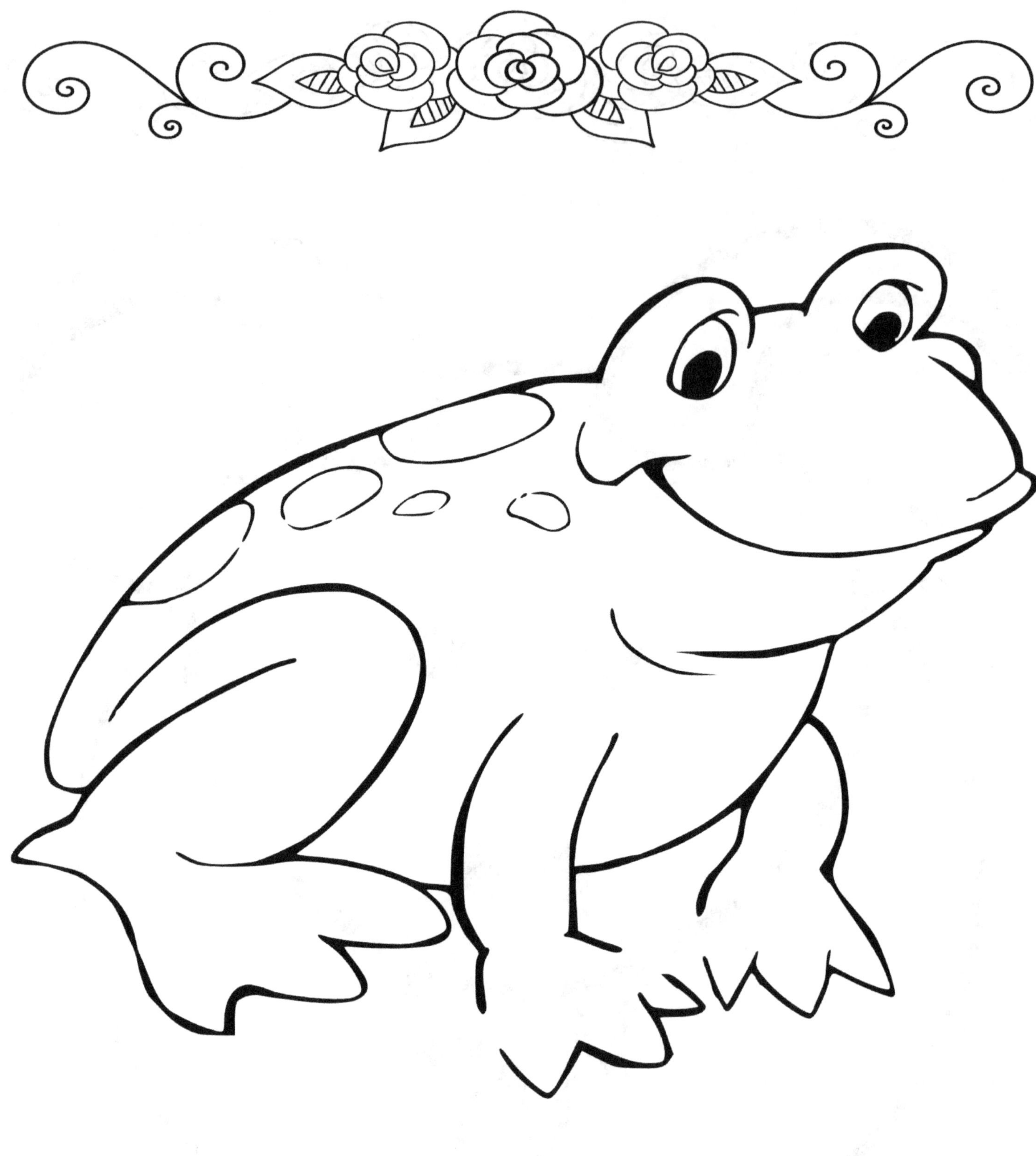

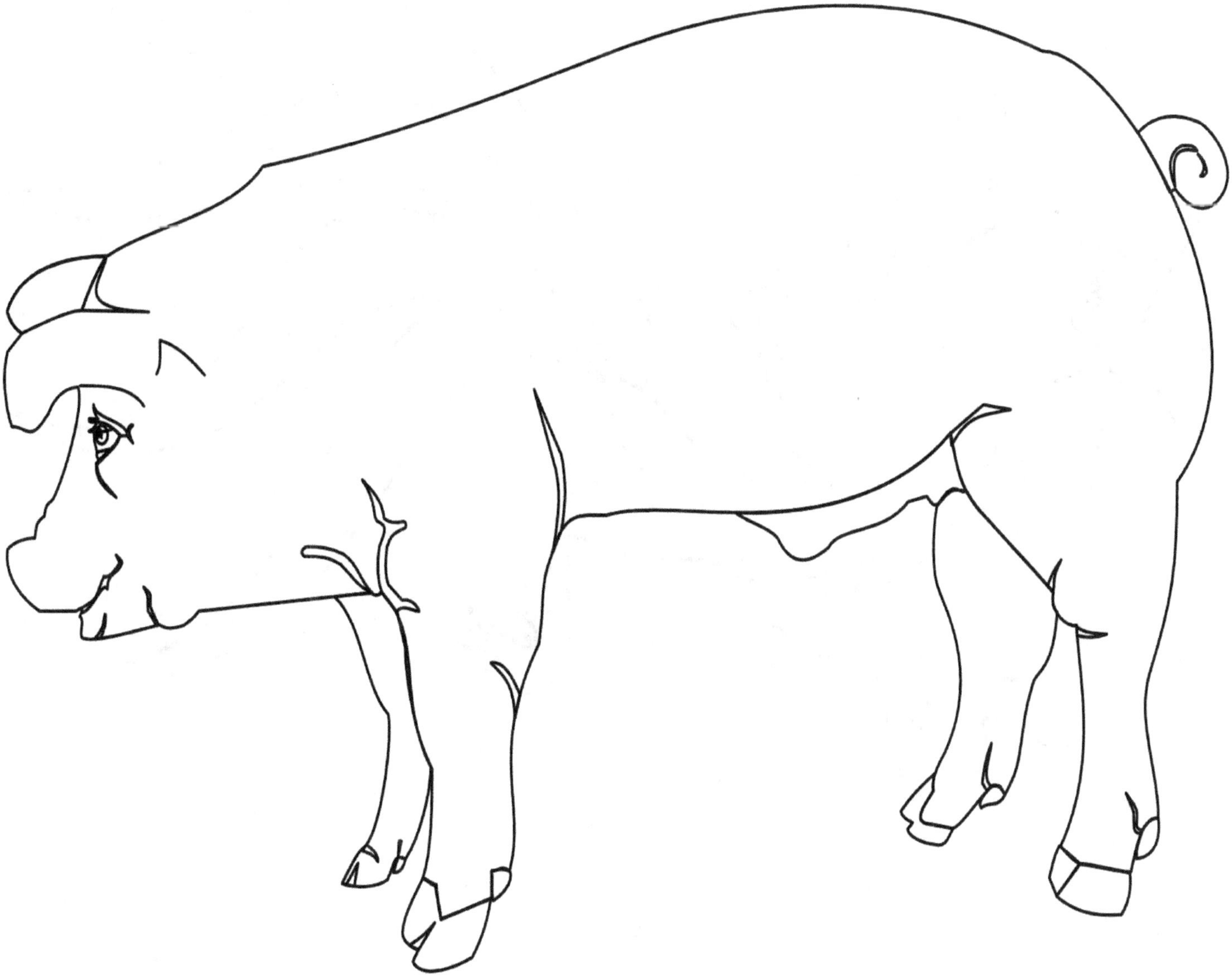

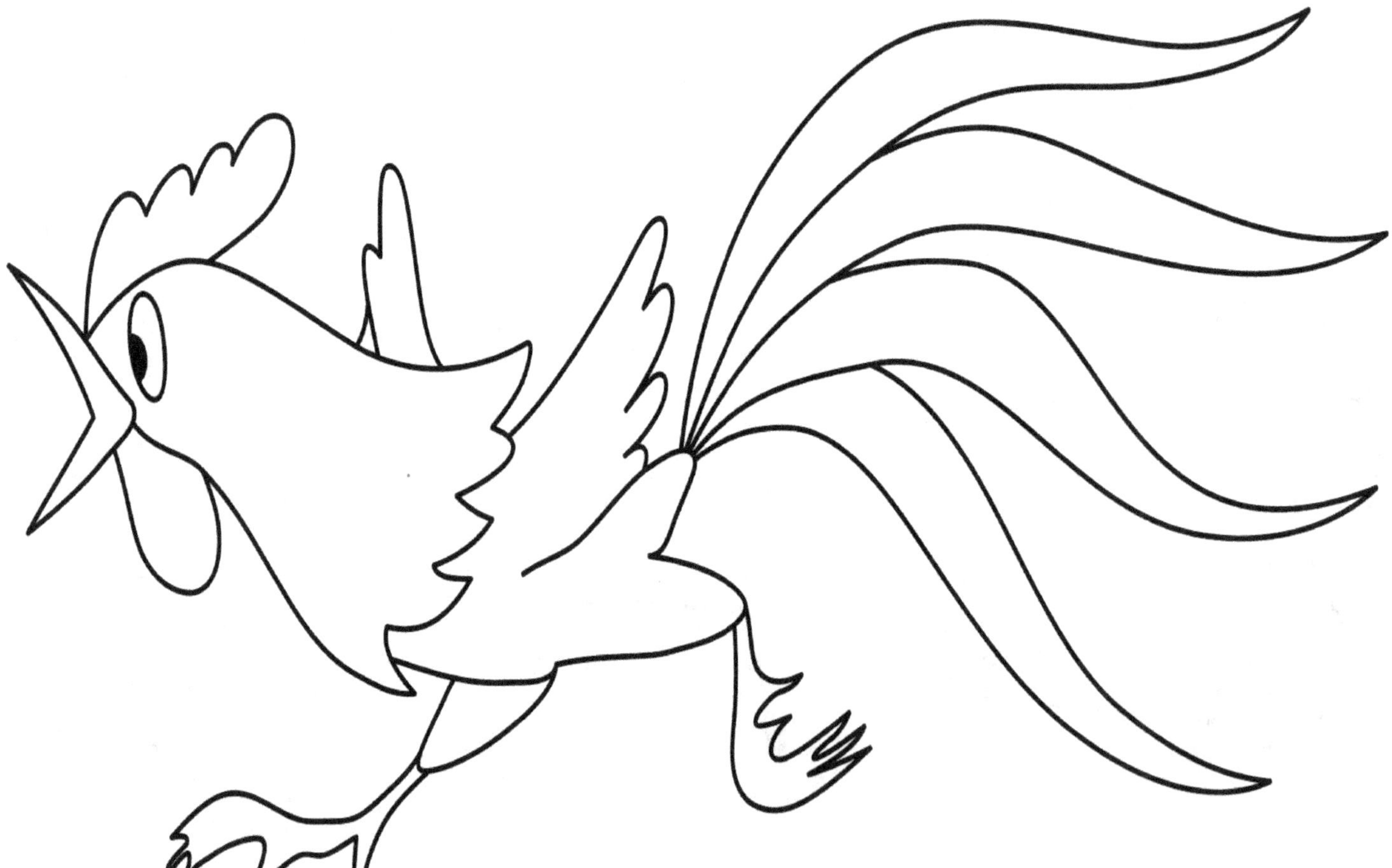

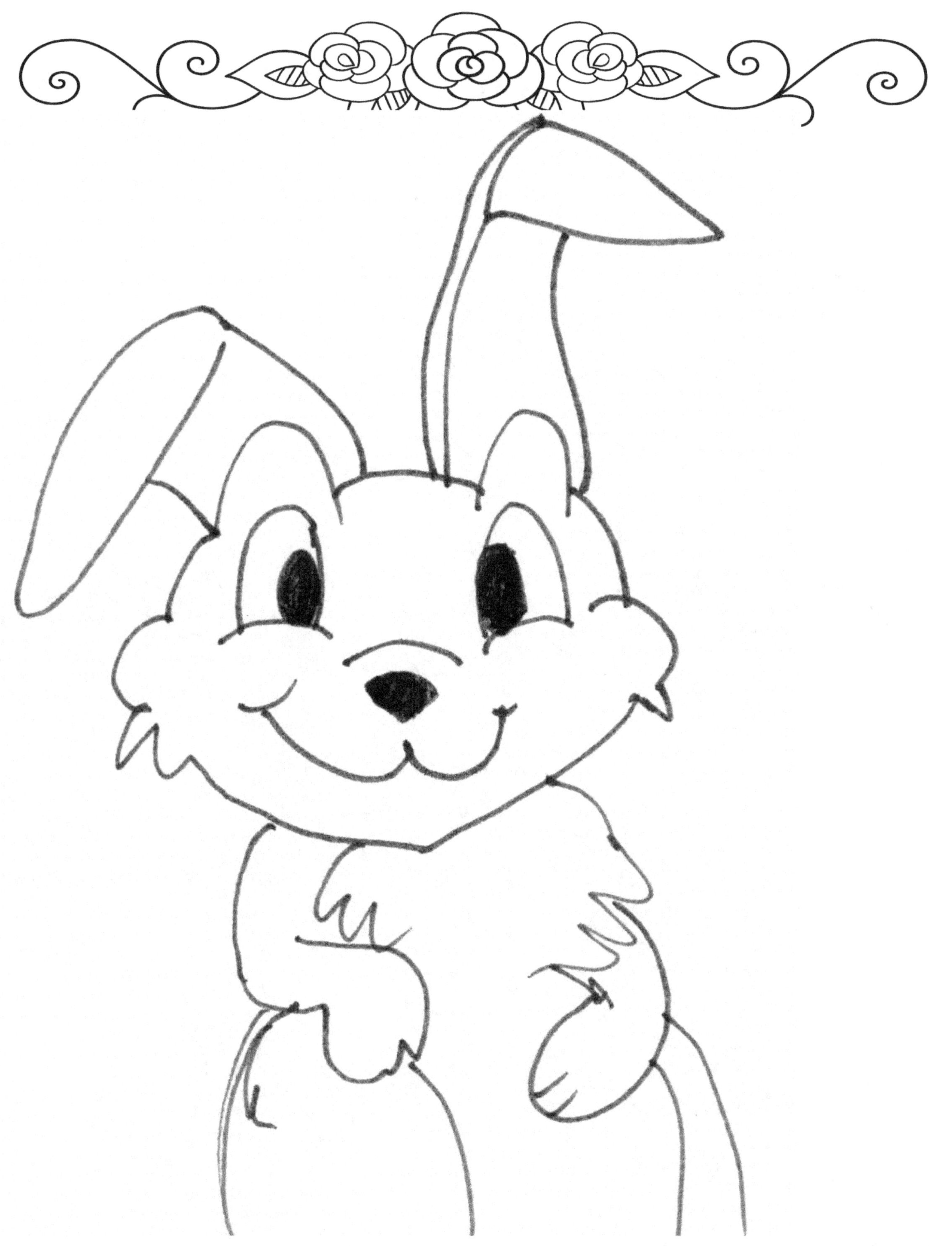

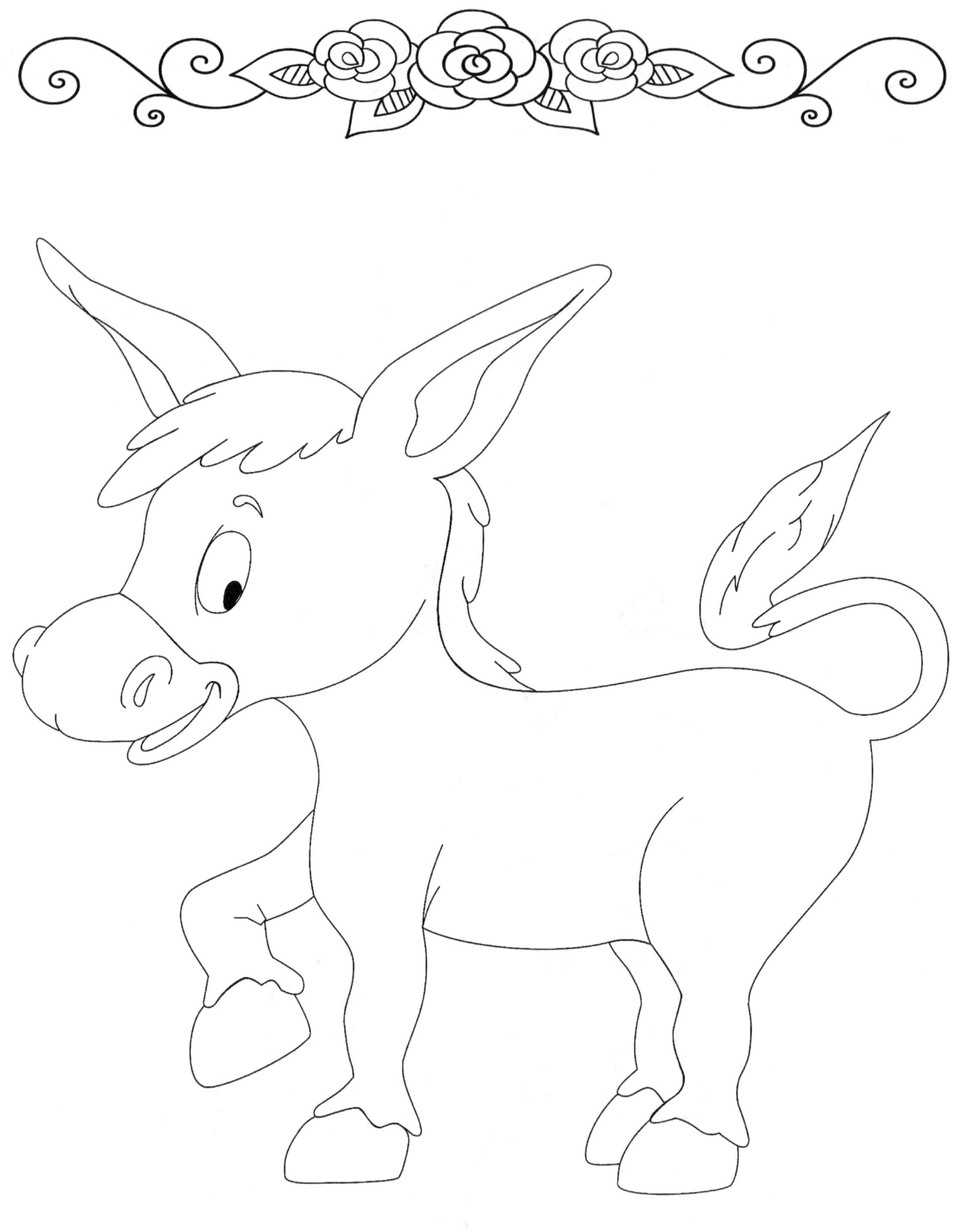

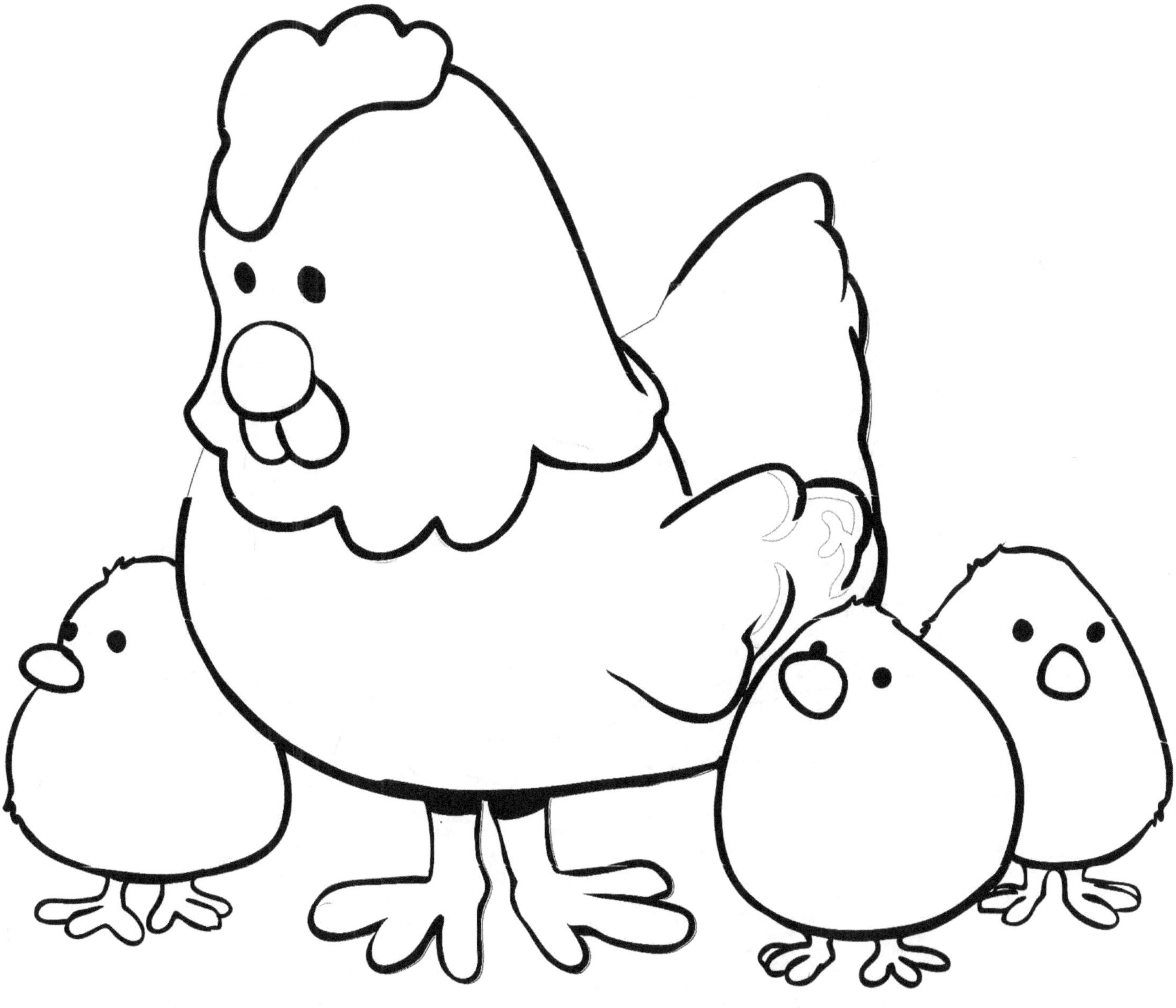

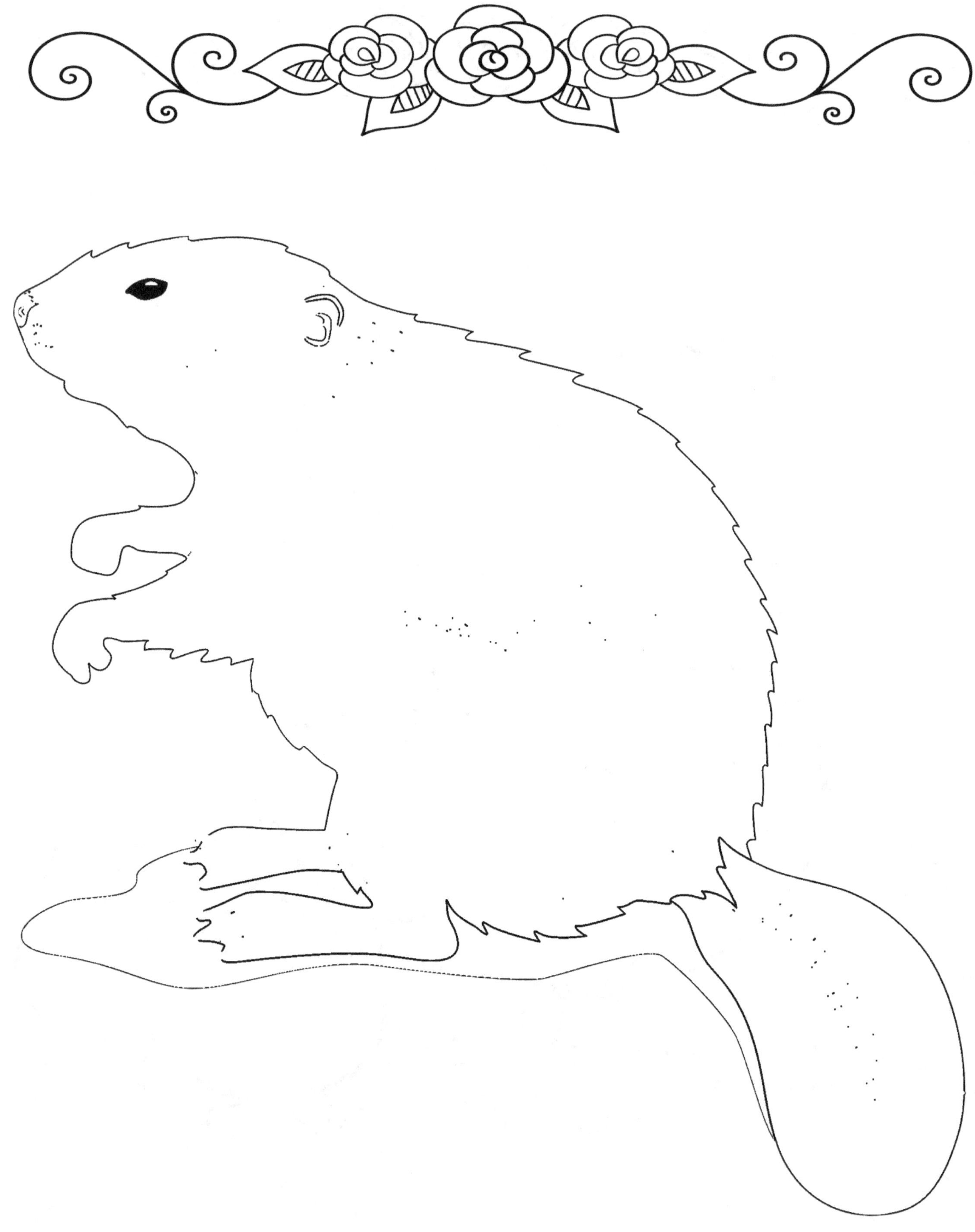

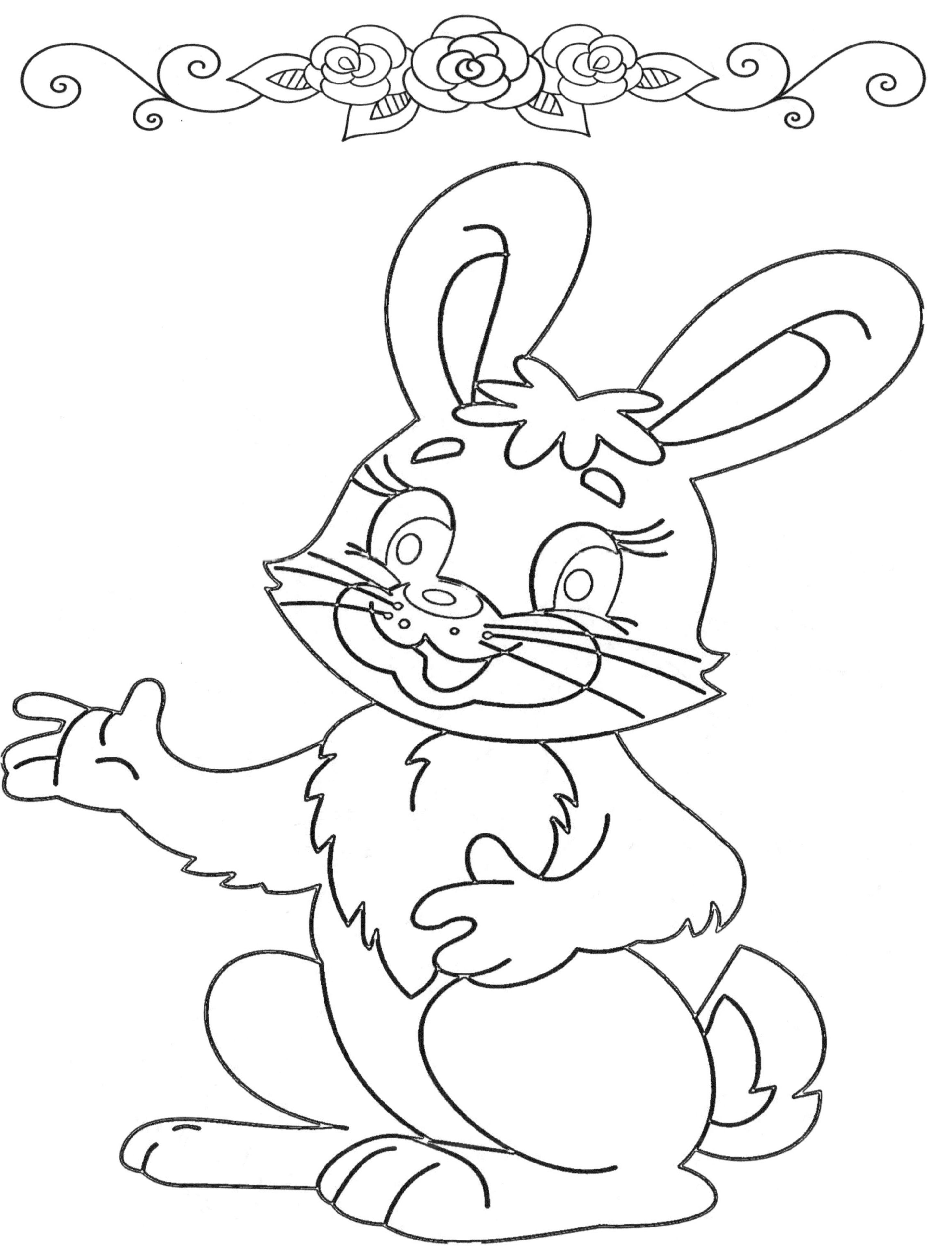

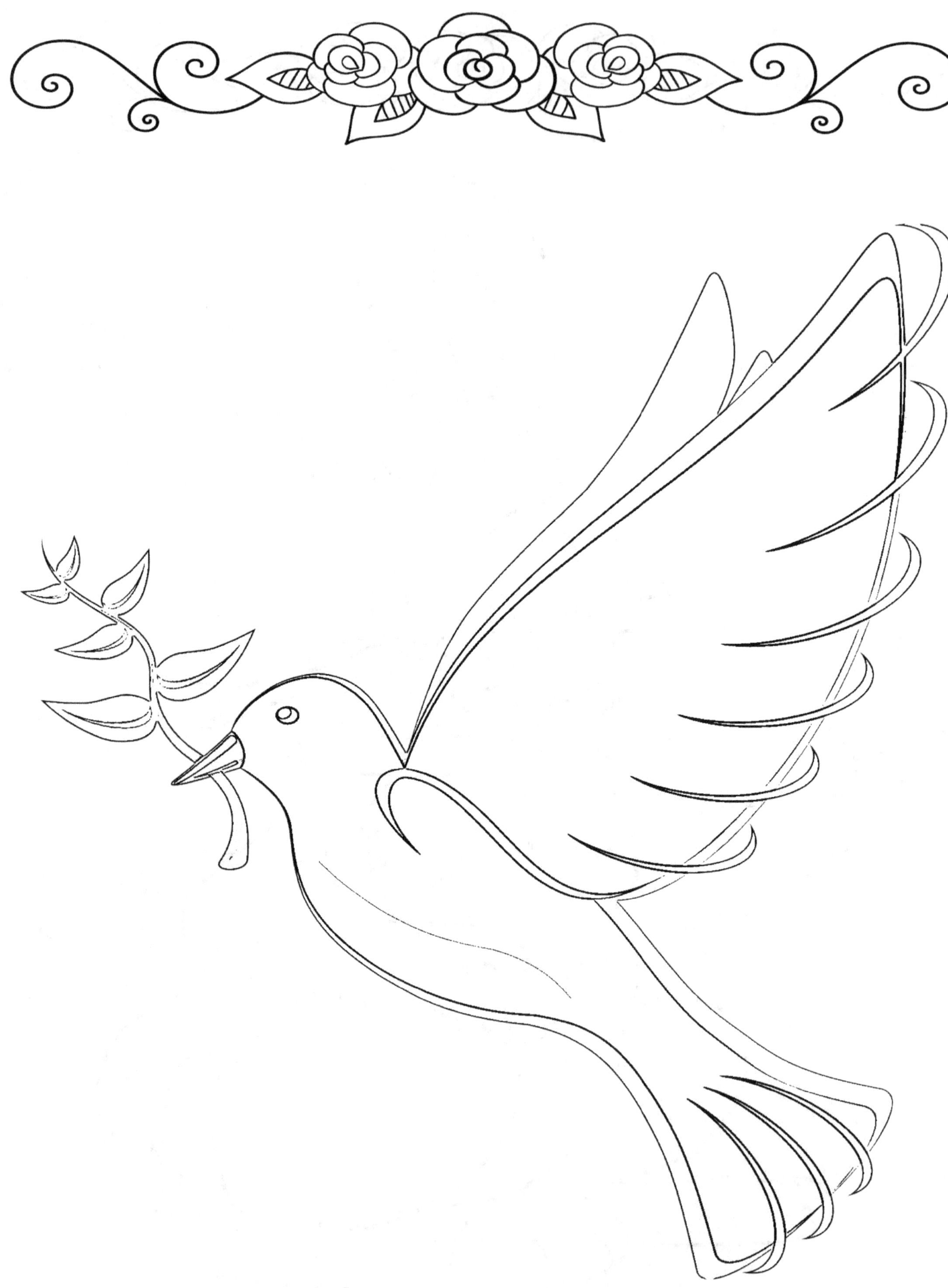

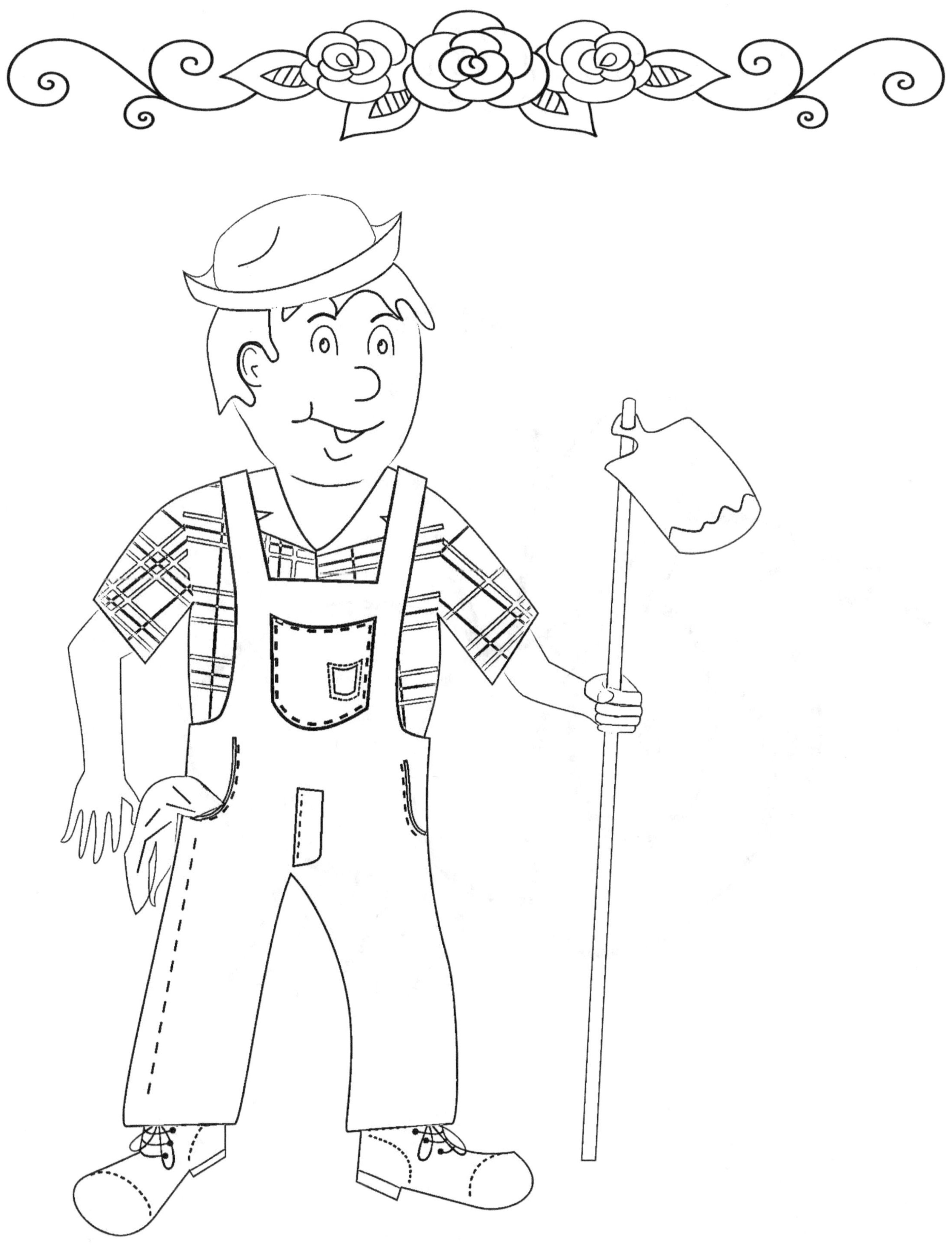

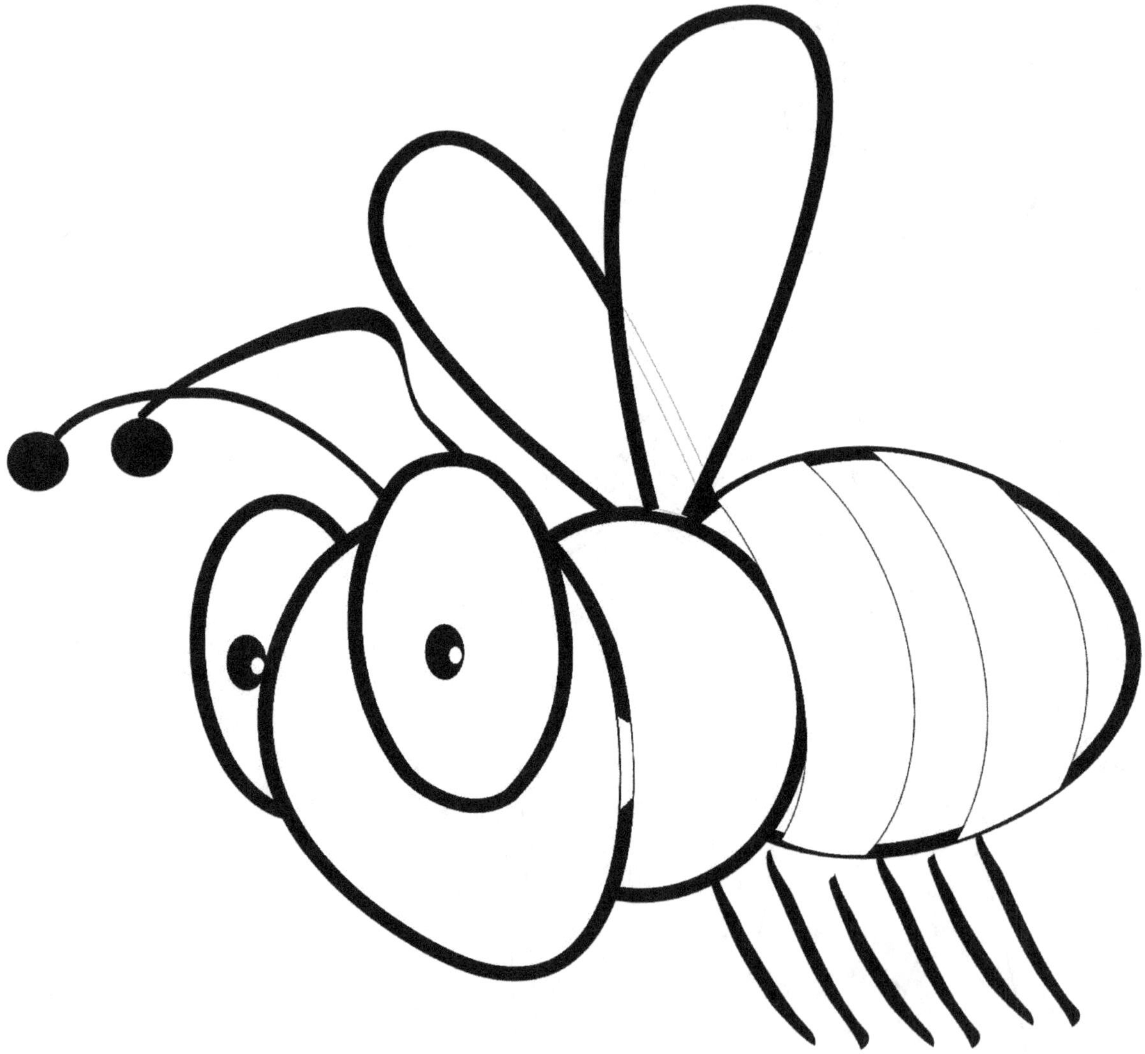

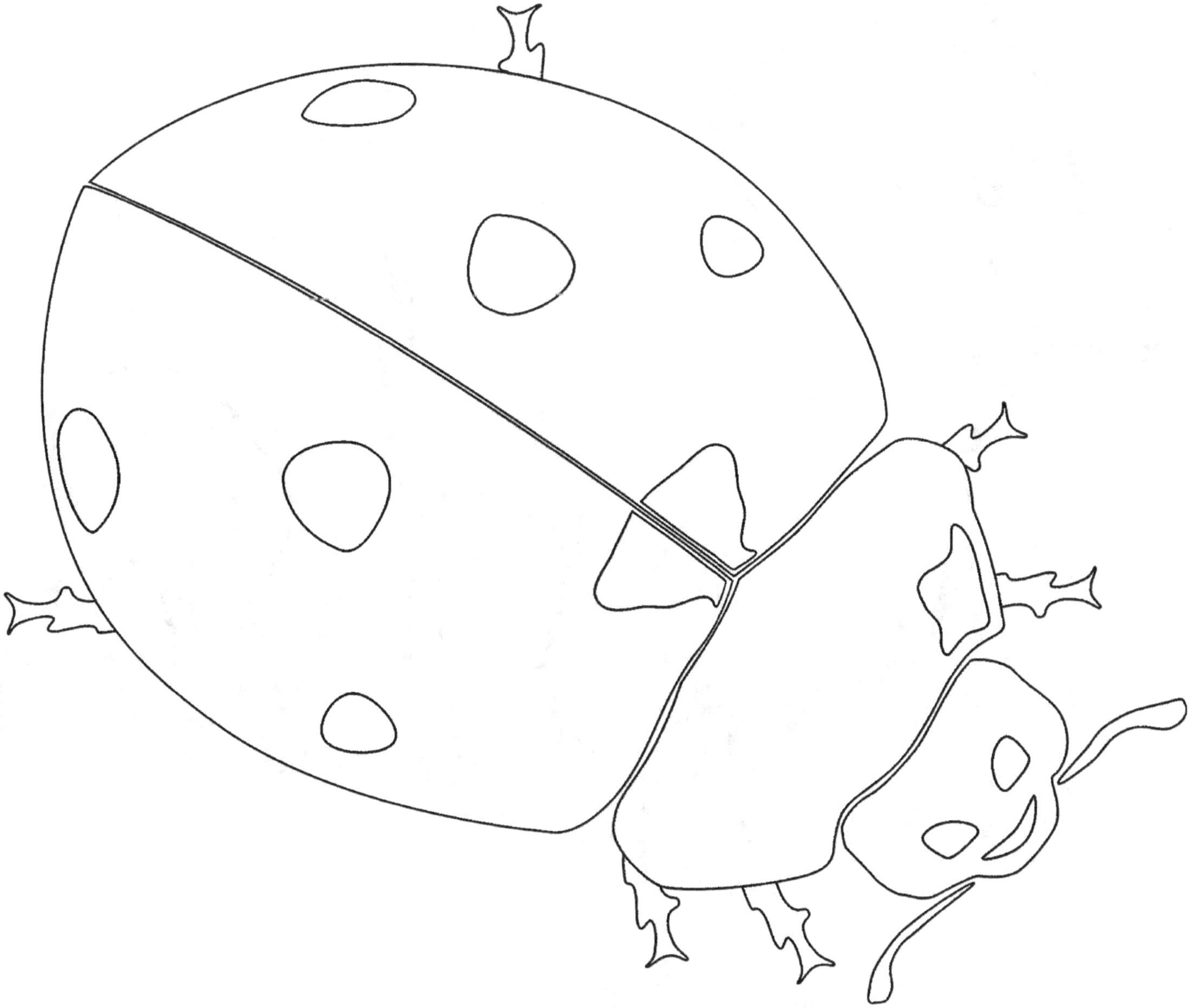

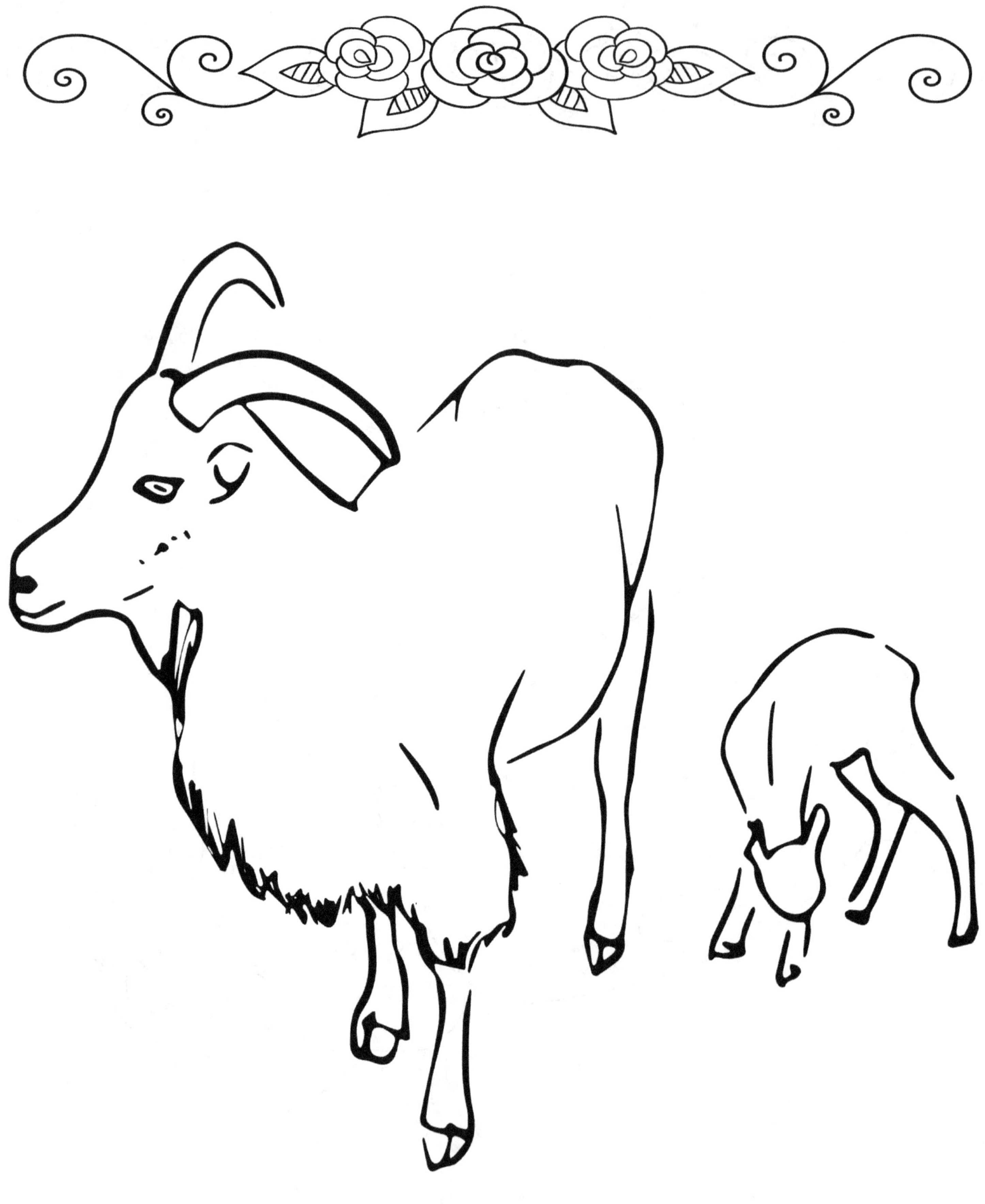

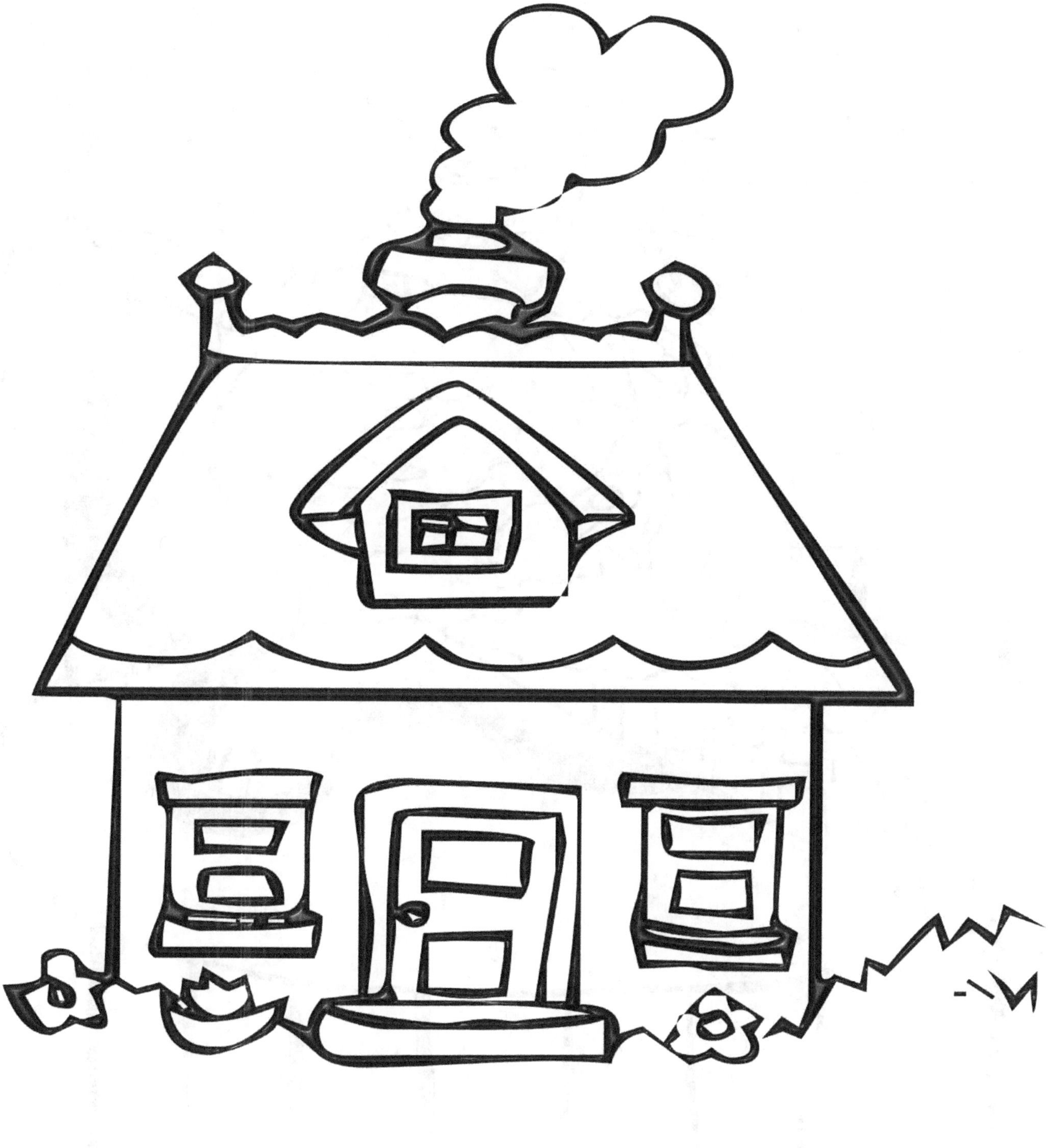

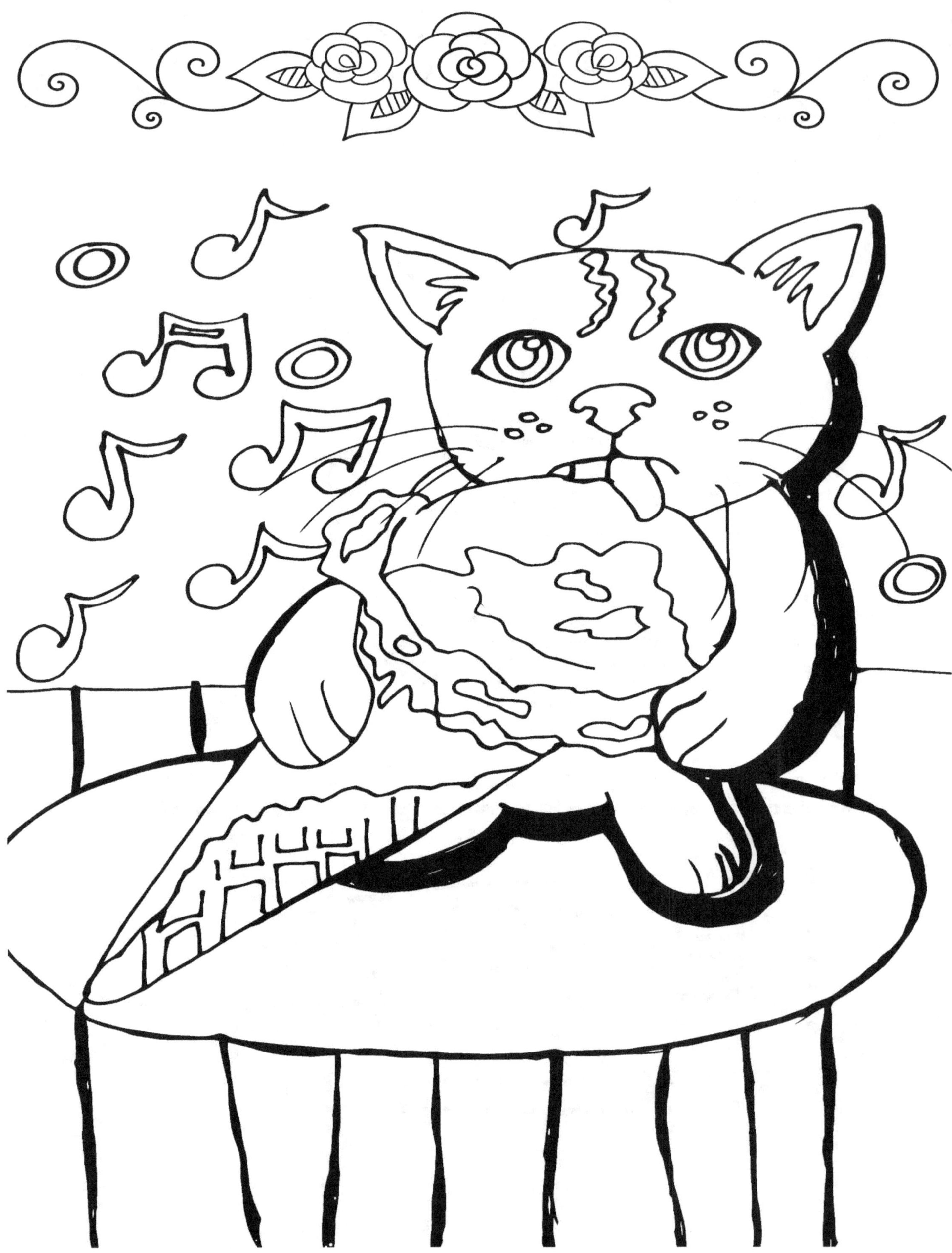

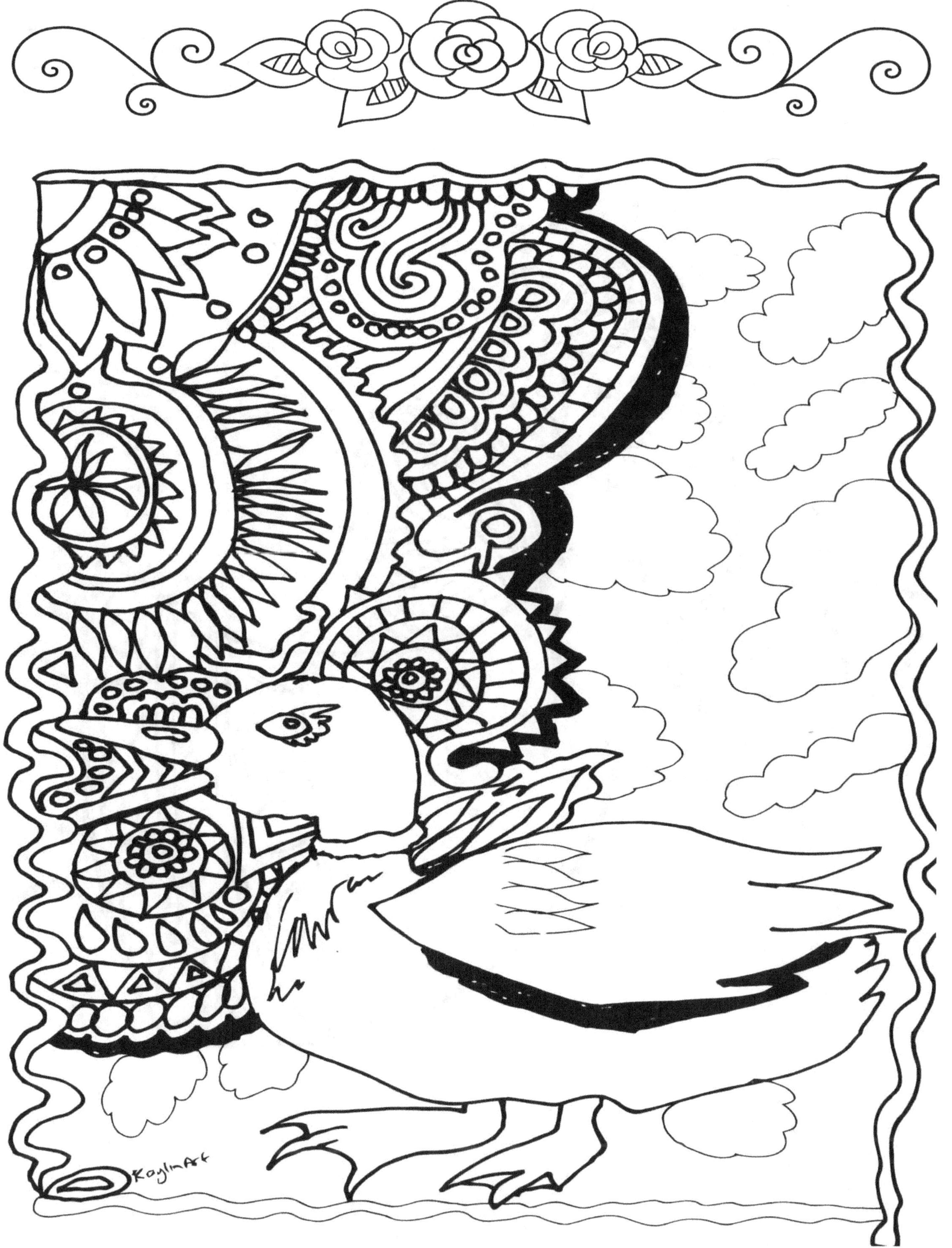
KaylinArt

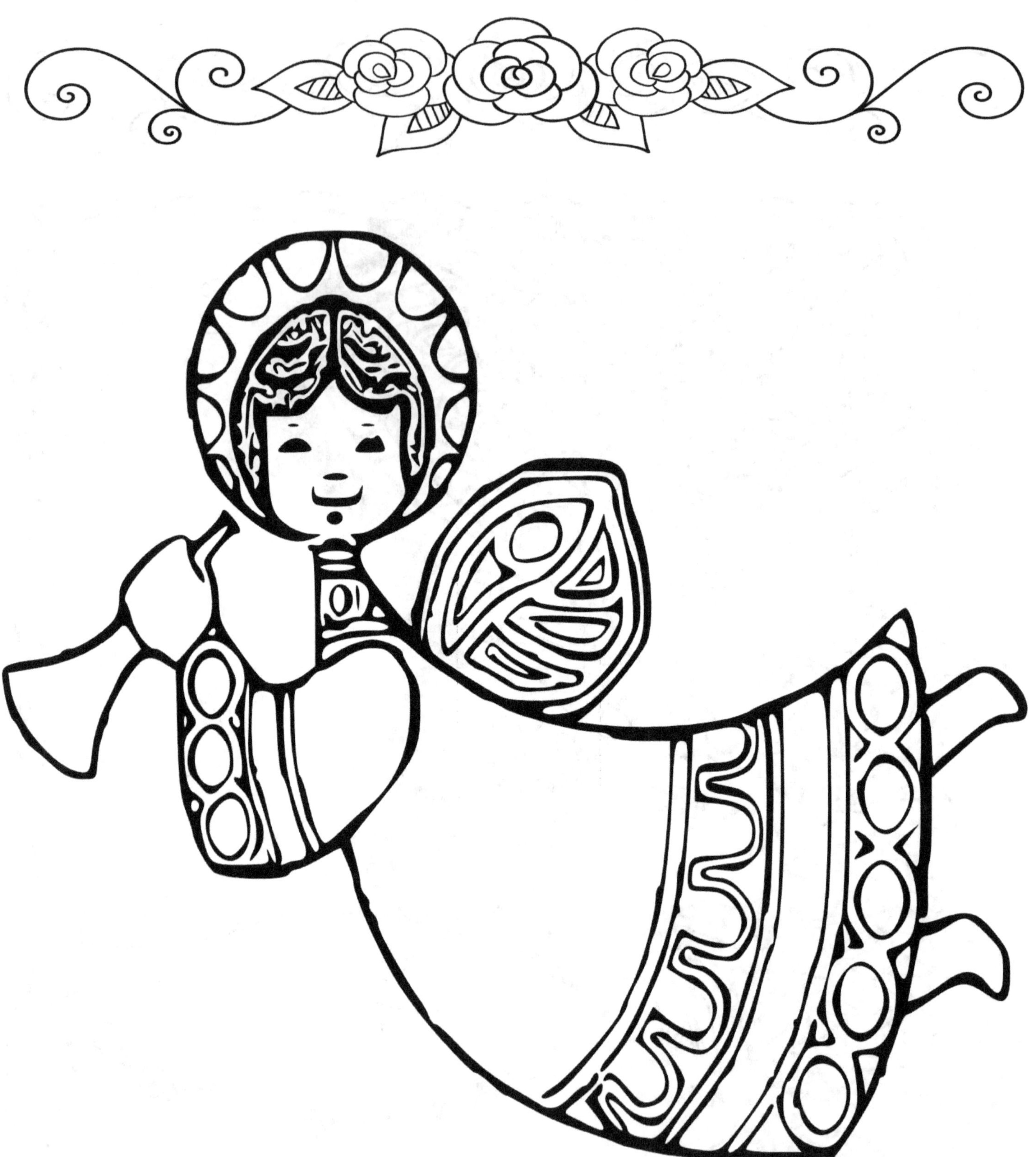

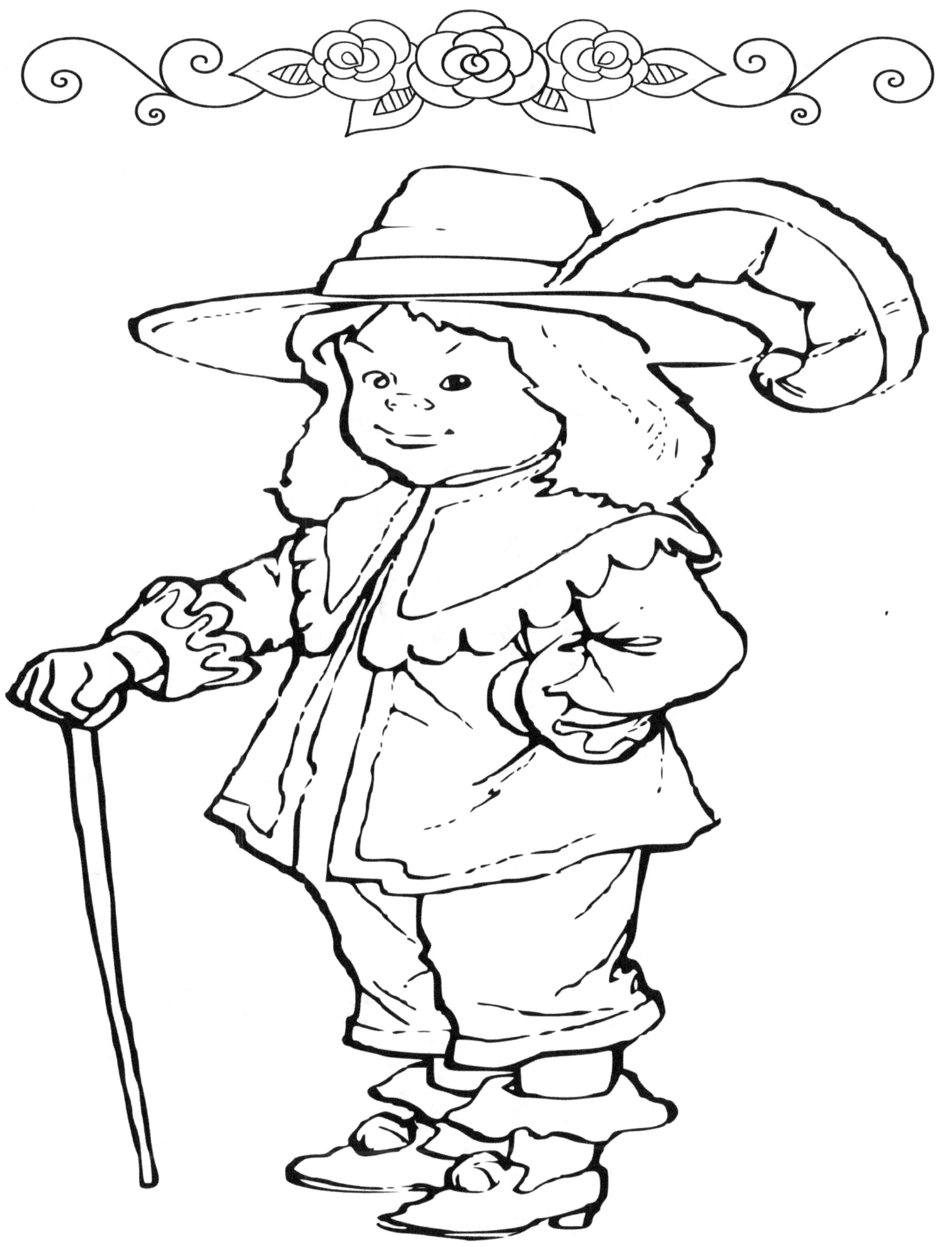

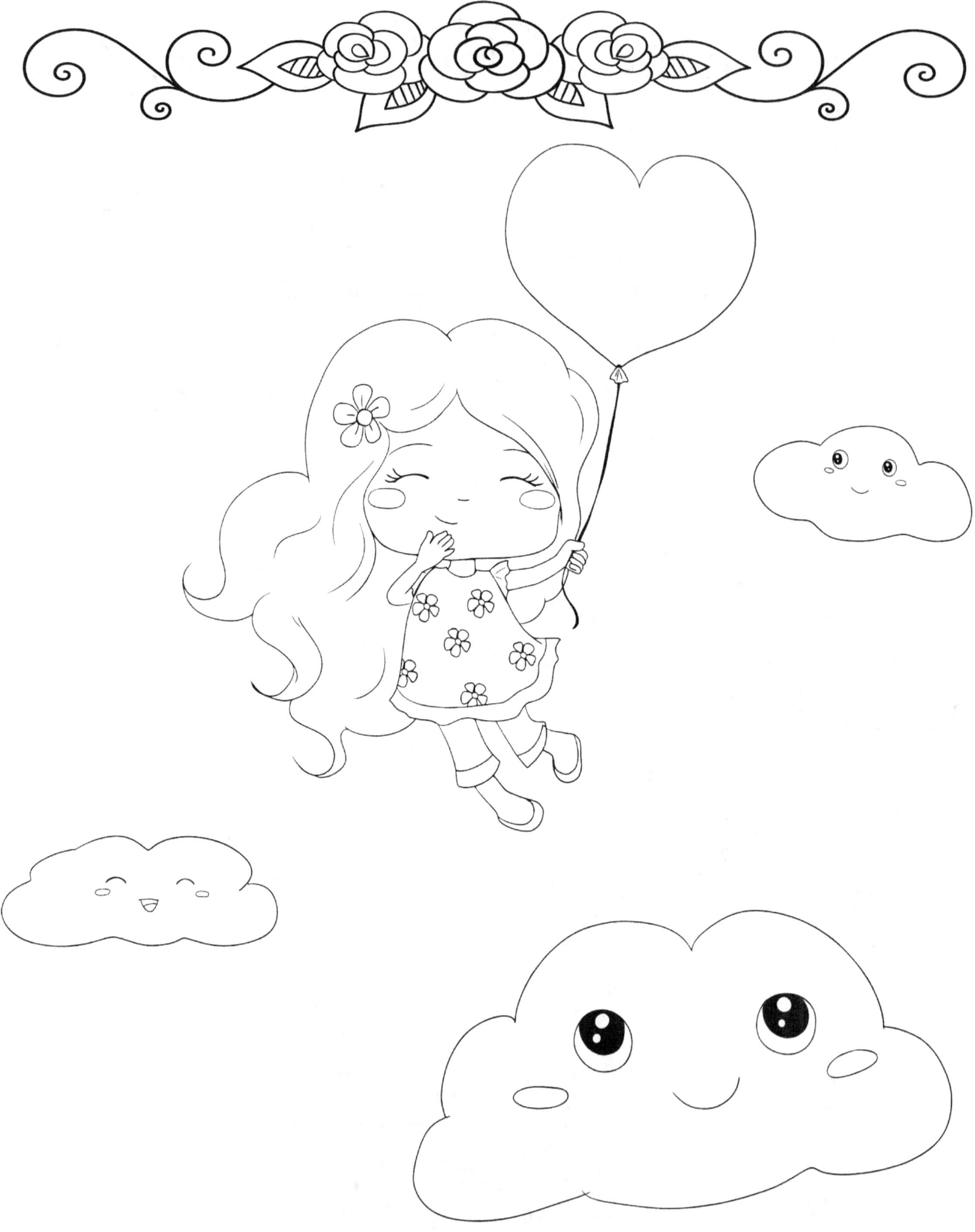

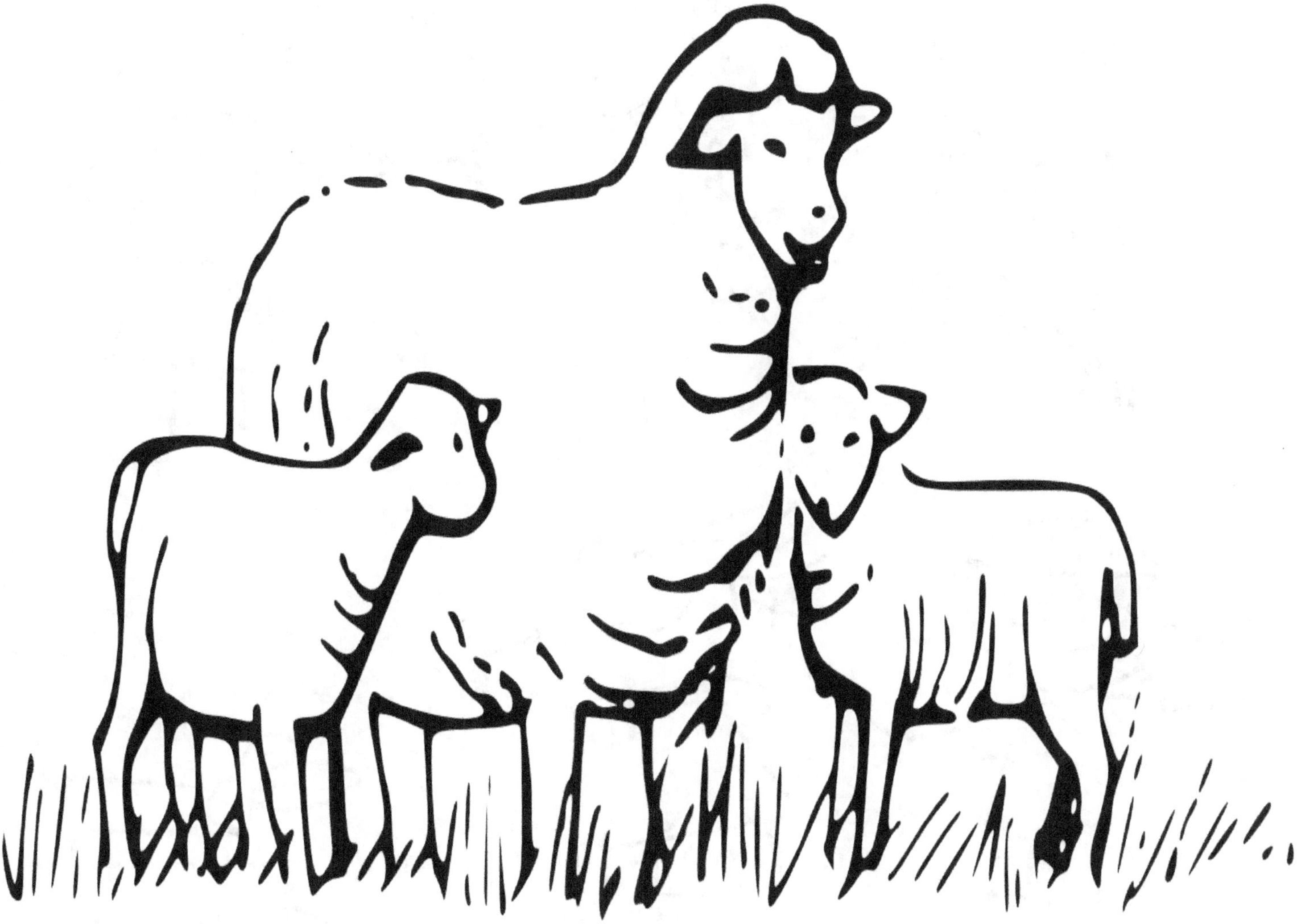

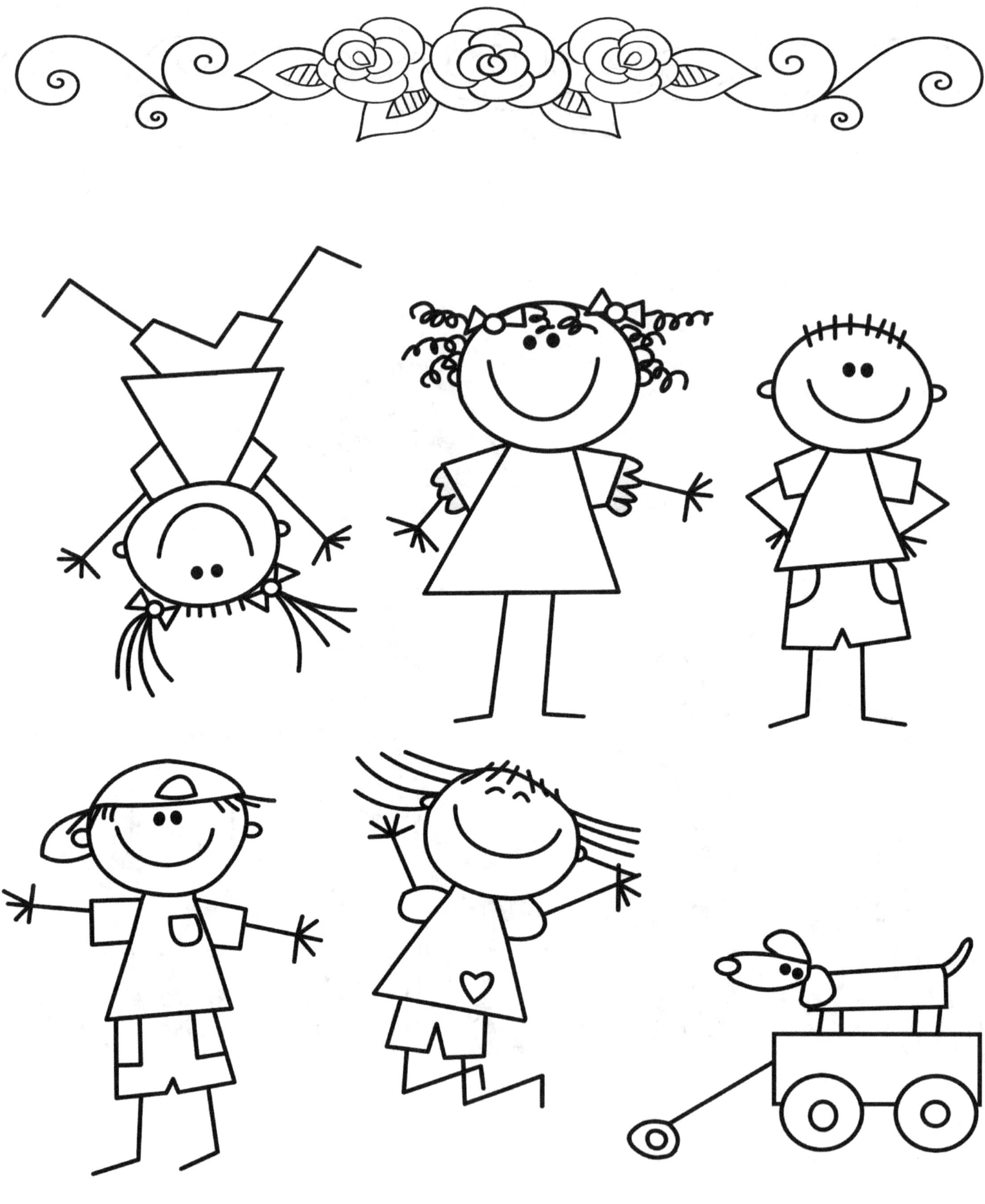

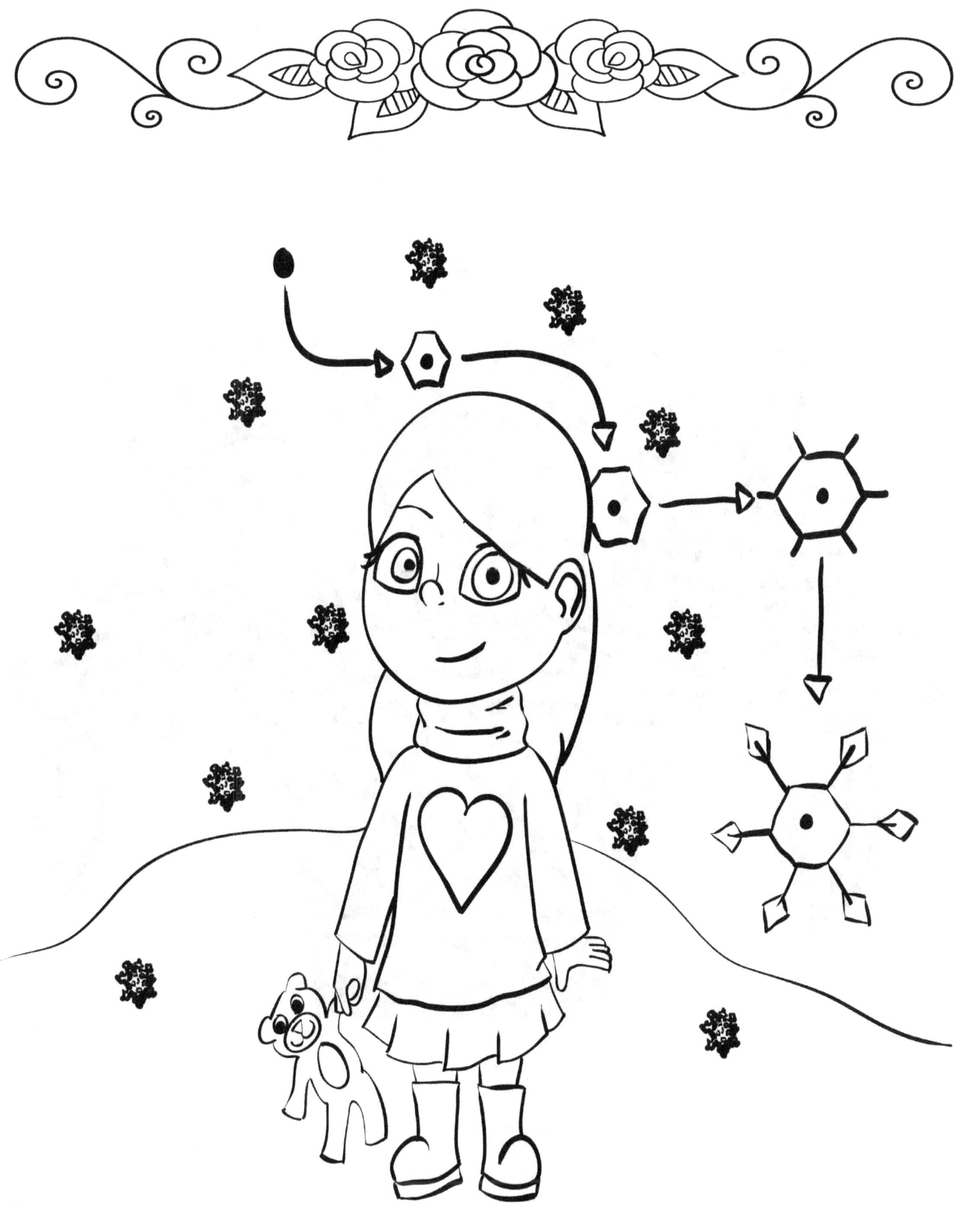

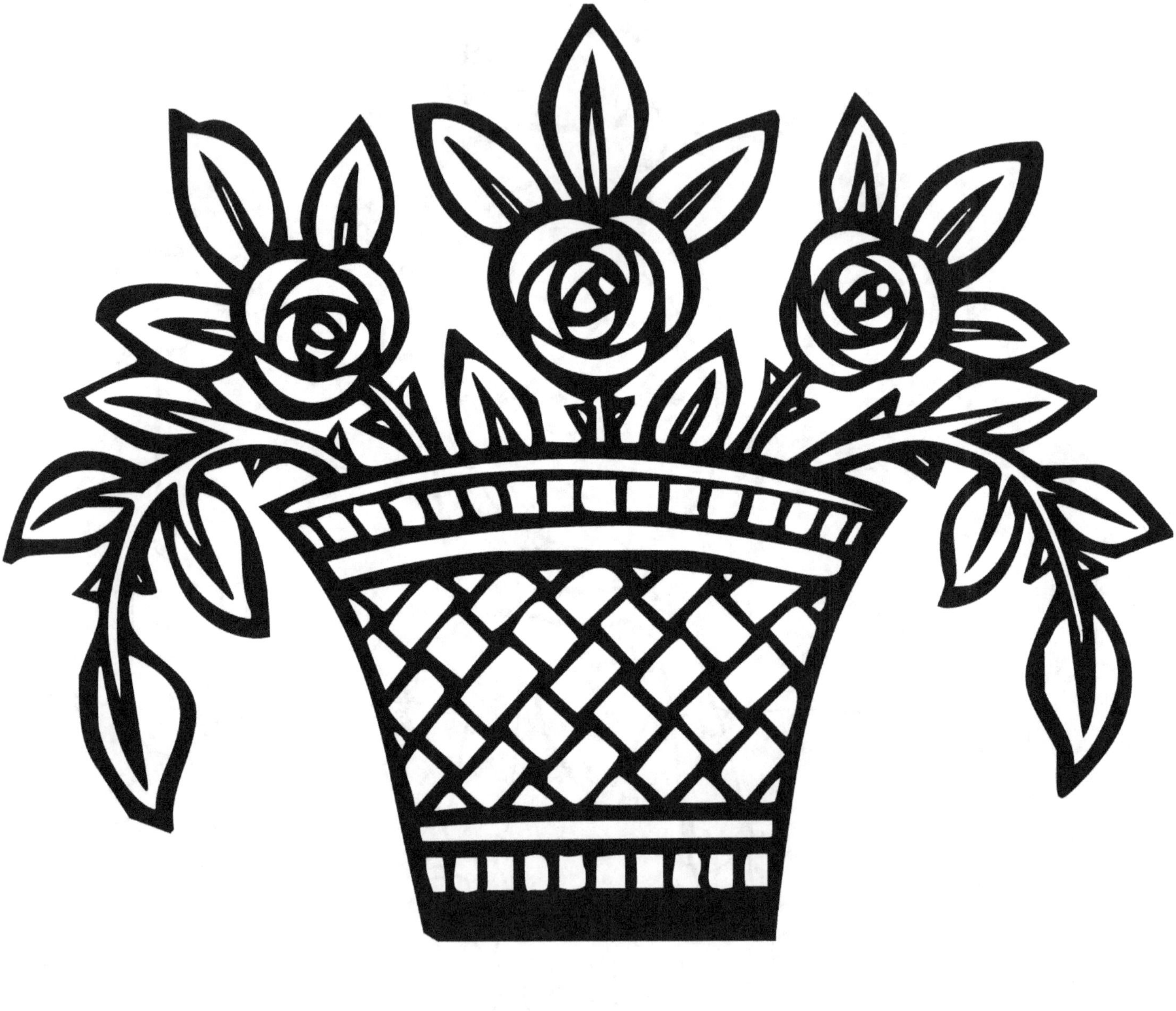

www.ingramcontent.com/pod-product-compliance
Lightning Source LLC
Chambersburg PA
CBHW081452250726
48662CB00009B/3049